Cambridge Elements ≡

Elements in the Philosophy of Mind
edited by
Keith Frankish
The University of Sheffield

BIOLOGICAL COGNITION

Bryce Huebner
Georgetown University

Jay Schulkin
University of Washington

CAMBRIDGE
UNIVERSITY PRESS

CAMBRIDGE
UNIVERSITY PRESS

Shaftesbury Road, Cambridge CB2 8EA, United Kingdom

One Liberty Plaza, 20th Floor, New York, NY 10006, USA

477 Williamstown Road, Port Melbourne, VIC 3207, Australia

314–321, 3rd Floor, Plot 3, Splendor Forum, Jasola District Centre,
New Delhi – 110025, India

103 Penang Road, #05-06/07, Visioncrest Commercial, Singapore 238467

Cambridge University Press is part of Cambridge University Press & Assessment,
a department of the University of Cambridge.

We share the University's mission to contribute to society through the pursuit of
education, learning and research at the highest international levels of excellence.

www.cambridge.org
Information on this title: www.cambridge.org/9781108987059

DOI: 10.1017/9781108982191

First published 2022

A catalogue record for this publication is available from the British Library.

ISBN 978-1-108-98705-9 Paperback
ISSN 2633-9080 (online)
ISSN 2633-9072 (print)

Biological Cognition

Elements in the Philosophy of Mind

DOI: 10.1017/9781108982191
First published online: November 2022

Bryce Huebner
Georgetown University

Jay Schulkin
University of Washington

Author for correspondence: Bryce Huebner,
bryce.huebner@georgetown.edu

Abstract: This Element introduces a biological approach to cognition, which highlights the significance of allostatic regulation and the navigation of challenges and opportunities. It argues that cognition is best understood as a juggling act, which reflects numerous ongoing attempts to minimize disruptions while prioritizing the sources of information that are necessary to satisfy social and biological needs; and it provides a characterization of the architectural constraints, neurotransmitters, and affective states that shape visual perception, as well as the regulatory capacities that sustain flexible patterns of thought and behavior.

Keywords: allostasis, adaptive behavior, vision, learning, chemical signaling systems

ISBNs: 9781108987059 (PB), 9781108982191 (OC)
ISSNs: 2633-9080 (online), 2633-9072 (print)

Contents

1 Introduction

Cognitive scientists often note that neural networks *can be* organized to implement logical operations and execute logical functions. Some hypothesize that cognition is implemented directly by parallel processing algorithms that modify the connection weights within neural networks. Others claim that cognition is a matter of implicit symbol manipulation that exploits inferential operations that are implemented by neural logic gates. Each of these approaches has advanced our collective understanding of cognition and experience. But there is an approach to biological cognition that is less familiar and that highlights the diverse range of processes that are employed as animals navigate *biological and social challenges* to *preserve viability*.

Preserving viability often requires locating nutritional resources and remembering where they can be found, while avoiding predation and pursuing social support. These forms of cognition always unfold against the backdrop of metabolic demands that must be managed for an animal to survive and flourish. In complex and dangerous environments, this will often require tracking the likelihood of various risks and threats; an animal's sensitivity to these risks and threats will often be shaped by everything from the consequences of managing recent challenges to their histories of past trauma. Just as importantly, the demands that arise in contexts like breeding, pregnancy, and lactation, as well as the management of hunger and thirst, can shift the features of the world that are most salient to an animal. So, a plausible story about cognition must explain how animals are able to respond to sustained patterns of resource availability, adjust their behavior in light of current and anticipated needs, and manage fluctuations in bodily, ecological, and social variables.

There is no doubt that such capacities are organized by nervous systems in all mobile animals. But a precise and general account of the biological processes that sustain adaptive behavior has proven elusive. There are observable regularities in neural processes that are modulated by various chemical systems. But adjustments to one process often evoke changes in other processes as animals respond to biological challenges, prioritize physiological and social needs, weigh opportunities, and establish efficient trade-offs between diverse behavioral and cognitive strategies. Consequently, a biological approach to cognition must move beyond simplified forms of functionalism that attempt to establish the neurally based causal relations that instantiate familiar categories like beliefs, desires, and thoughts in two ways: (1) it must provide a characterization of the ecological and physiological constraints that organize *strategies for managing specific challenges and opportunities*; and (2) it must highlight the embodied strategies that animals internalize as they learn to manage predictable and unpredictable changes in access to things like food, water, minerals, and social support. Critically, this preserves a commitment to an empirically grounded form of functionalism, according to which the neural, chemical, and ecological phenomena that constitute animal minds are to be understood in terms of the causal roles that they play in guiding thought and behavior, as well as producing experiences of various challenges and opportunities.

Given these considerations, we will not defend an approach to cognition that is grounded in commonsense- or folk-psychology in this Element. Nor will we develop a priori claims about the nature of the mind. Instead, we will pursue a naturalistic approach to biological cognition that preserves a tight connection to data and methods from the cognitive and biological sciences. In this respect, our approach diverges from recent defenses of philosophical empiricism that have garnered support from results in machine learning (Buckner 2018). Such approaches suggest that domain-general forms of learning and abstraction suffice to explain all of the diverse capacities that are observed in cognitive systems. We disagree. But this is not because we accept a form of philosophical nativism that is anchored to traditional taxonomies of mental phenomena. We acknowledge that some cognitive capacities are resilient to differences in learning environments, and this is a point that we return to in the closing section of this element. Furthermore, as we argue in Section 3, there are cases where one-trial learning suggests that animals are biologically prepared to learn about specific domains of phenomena. But far more generally, we think that understanding *biological cognition* requires exploring the ways that ecological and physiological constraints shape the flow of information through embodied, situated, and complex biological systems. At many points, we will thus appeal directly to physiological considerations. We hope that this will clarify the roles that evolution and development can play in shaping cognition, while leaving room for diverse cognitive strategies to arise as animals manage ecologically and socially significant challenges. But to get a sense of what this means, it will help to consider the kinds of questions that arise when we focus on encouters with challenges and opportunities, in the context of preserving viability.

In the remainder of this introductory section, we thus provide a high-level overview of the kind of cognitive architecture that supports biological cognition. We then explore the implications of adopting this approach in the context of visual perception, a context where the importance of a biological perspective is likely to be clear to many philosophers and cognitive scientists (Section 2). We then turn to questions about learning and social cognition (Section 3 and Section 4), and we conclude with a brief discussion of how this approach might shape future inquiries in the cognitive sciences (Section 5). To ease into this approach, however, let's begin by considering the behavior of free-roaming elephants (Figure 1).

Figure 1 A small family of elephants.
Public domain image, Elephant Family in Tanzania, Wikimedia Commons.

1.1 Preserving Viability

Elephants are large animals who cover long distances in search of nutritional resources (Bates et al. 2008; Bradshaw 2009). They must eat huge quantities of plants and fruit to survive, and they spend most of the day foraging. But they don't do so randomly; they display a pronounced sensitivity to the demands of competition with other herbivores and other groups of elephants. They must also access substantial volumes of water, and elephants sometimes dig wells and cover them over so other animals will not find them. Finally, elephants must seek out minerals such as salt that are necessary for survival but difficult to obtain in sufficient quantities; in one striking example, elephants who found a high-quality salt mine followed remembered routes to this mine for many years, adjusting their timing and strategies when challenges to their survival and well-being emerged (Schulkin 1991).

Elephants are also highly social animals, and their lives are organized by lasting friendships, robust family bonds, and patterns of alloparenting (Archie et al. 2011). They also communicate in diverse ways to manage challenges and opportunities collectively. Over short distances, they use approximately thirty different calls and eighty visual and tactile displays; over long distances, they use low-frequency vocalizations, which can be detected as sounds and vibrations. These long-range vocalizations can be used to alert distant elephants to the presence of various challenges and opportunities, including the presence of predators. Few predators (other than humans) will attack elephants. But, in recent years, the ability of elephants to call out to others has had disastrous effects. Poachers will sometimes kill off the mature elephants in a herd and wait for other elephants to arrive in response to these long-range calls. The result is that huge numbers of mature elephants are killed, and many young elephants end up witnessing their entire herds being killed off.

Human activity has brought about robust changes in resource availability, alongside these extreme disruptions of elephant social relationships, so many elephants have developed novel cognitive and affective strategies for managing human-generated challenges. For example, the salt-mining elephants that we mentioned above must cope with a pervasive fear of poachers, who sometimes wait for them to arrive at the salt mine; and animals who have witnessed the violent deaths of their herds experience anxiety and distress, as well as heightened patterns of anticipatory aggression. Some of these traumatized elephants engage in uncharacteristically aggressive behavior within their communities; others direct hostility toward humans and other animals. But just as strikingly, many of these elephants have developed capacities to track the subtle cues that indicate human group membership, such as clothing and scent, and they are more vigilant after experiencing cues associated with the groups who tend to attack them. Finally, there is suggestive evidence that social regulation, driven by interactions between adolescent males and less-traumatized bulls, can sometimes mitigate the effects of past trauma (Bradshaw 2009).

To explain these patterns of experience and behavior, it is necessary to ask how elephants learn about their world while managing metabolic and social needs, as well as dealing with various form of stress and trauma. This requires looking beyond the kinds of information that can be collected in a laboratory environment, and it requires looking beyond simple appeals to beliefs, desires, or other categories that are commonly discussed by philosophers. Specifically, it requires examining: (1) the physiological processes that are employed as elephants anticipate changes in internal and external states; (2) the strategies they employ to accommodate anticipated changes using chemical signaling systems; and (3) the changes in physiological and hormonal regulation that arise and persist in the wake of trauma, yielding pronounced changes in the elephant's willingness to seek social support (Bradshaw & Schore 2007).

By highlighting processes that organize responses to *biological challenges and opportunities*, an approach to cognition that highlights *allostatic* regulation comes into view. An 'allostatic system' attempts to preserve viability through change, and 'allostatic regulation' is the process by which animals adjust and adapt to changing circumstances, often using diverse forms of anticipatory regulation to coordinate diverse bodily systems. A biological approach to cognition that centers allostatic regulation reveals a wide range of information-processing strategies that are involved in producing and regulating behavior, as well as managing physiological and social challenges (compare Allen 2017; Heyes 2019). These information-processing strategies are sustained by forms of analog and digital signal manipulation, which are implemented by neural and chemical signaling systems, and they are supported by diverse forms of affect, which organize perception and learning. But just as importantly, a biological approach to cognition must accept a kind of *embodied pluralism* that is sensitive to the way that various challenges and opportunities affect embodiment, experience, cognition, and behavior. The implications of this approach are wide ranging, or so we argue over the course of this Element. This approach entails that appeals to computational or representational considerations should be integrated within a broader account of how animals preserve viability through change, and it entails that claims about processes like remembering, planning, and linguistic processing must be situated within an account of how animals navigate the physiological and social challenges that they face.

1.2 Embodiment as a Core Principle of Biological Cognition

An influential understanding of this form of *embodied pluralism* was articulated by Claude Bernard. Building on his knowledge of digestive enzymes, glucose synthesis, and the response of blood vessels to changes in temperature, he hypothesized that regulating the internal milieu was essential to life, and he argued that biological systems always have the purpose "of maintaining the integrity of the conditions for life in the internal environment" (Bernard 1974, 89). Bernard was not primarily concerned with mentality or cognition, but Ivan Pavlov (1927) extended the claim that biological systems preserve viability by regulating their internal milieu to questions about learning and decision-making, exploring the ways that animals adapt to contextual changes. He showed, for example, that interactions between the brain and digestive glands support a form of adaptive learning, where *anticipating* food passing through the oral cavity triggers insulin secretion, preparing the animal to absorb vital nutrients. This was a significant advance because it showed that a cognitive state could use a chemical signal to organize system-level behavior, while the digestive glands could use that signal to shape experiences of hunger and satiation. Pavlov hypothesized that extensions of this approach could provide a basis for a scientifically grounded theory of 'psychic activity,' including a wide range of psychiatric phenomena.

Drawing upon Pavlov's research, Ernest Starling (1905) examined a diverse range of chemical signals that could carry information through the bloodstream to organize nervous activity and regulate various organs. He called these chemical messengers 'hormones' ('ὁρμάω,' 'setting in motion'), to highlight their role in exciting and arousing behavior. When his critical insights were taken up by Walter Cannon (1917, 1932), it became clear that there is a tight connection between the adrenal glands and the sympathetic nervous system. Cannon spent much of his career showing that the secretion of adrenaline played an important role in adaptive responses to deviations away from biological set-points, or desired states of critical biological variables. For example, he proposed that the 'flight-or-fight' response is regulated by neuroendocrine systems that motivate actions that would restore homeostasis through the management of biological or social challenges.

In the context of biological cognition, the management of biological and social challenges will always be complex. Recall the elephants who must track and respond to numerous variables, ranging from the availability of nutritional resources to the stability of their social communities and the likelihood that specific humans pose a threat to their continued survival. These elephants must manage access to water and minerals, and they must determine when it makes sense to seek social support. In doing so they employ diverse anticipatory control systems, which are responsive to: (1) variations in internal variables; (2) variations in the social, ecological, and physiological factors that constrain behavior; and (3) variations in the interactions between these diverse constraints (Bechtel 2009; Schulkin 2011). A wide range of brain-based systems *actively* monitor physiologically significant events; and they trigger anticipatory activity within diverse chemical signaling systems (including endocrine, neuroendocrine, and neurotransmitter systems), which play multiple roles in the organization of behavior, the management of uncertainty, and the preservation of viability.

Over the past several decades, it has become increasingly clear that numerous interacting processes are coordinated as animals confront various challenges and opportunities. These processes depend upon chemical signals, which operate over multiple timescales to organize behavior in response to changing needs for things like salt, glucose, water, and social acceptance; and they depend upon interactions between chemical and neural systems, which support the anticipation of challenges and opportunities, as well as the compensatory strategies that must be employed to preserve viability (McEwen 2004, 2007; Richter 1953; Sapolsky 1996; Schulkin 2004; Schulkin & Sterling 2019).

Research on these forms of physiological regulation have often focused on the forms of cognition that are employed in specific contexts, where specific chemical and neural processes are employed to cope with specific regulatory demands. But it is difficult to generalize from these precise and detailed explanations to the range of strategies that animals must employ as they accommodate shifting needs and priorities in naturalistic environments. This is a problem that commonly arises in biological contexts (Levins 1966; Odenbaugh 2003), but it will be crucial to keep this claim in mind over the course of this Element: the internal complexity and inherent variability of biological systems make it difficult to model behavior and physiological structure in ways that are precise, general, and biologically realistic, and these difficulties are exacerbated where a diverse array of biological and social constraints shape cognition in an ongoing way.

1.3 Pluralism about Processes

Animals must track potential dangers while monitoring fluctuations in metabolically significant resources and maintaining an awareness of where shelter and social relief are likely to be found. Likewise, many animals need to regulate social contact and social withdrawal in ways that allow them to manage social relationships. Finally, each of these processes must unfold as animals pursue some degree of 'predictive coherence' among the diverse processes that are dedicated to monitoring everything from the status of specific bodily tissues to the availability of resources and the structure of the social hierarchies that shape perception and learning (Schulkin 2015). Our claim about the difficulties inherent in modeling behavior and physiological structure in ways that are precise, general, and biologically realistic might therefore seem to make the study of cognition impossible.

However, it is important to note that many of the simple and low-cost forms of signal processing that manage the flow of bioelectric signals through neural networks are well understood. Some strategies for channeling the flow of activity are implemented directly by connections within neural networks, but more typically the activity of a neuron will be regulated by numerous chemical signals, which: (1) adjust the strength of connections between neurons; (2) affect the likelihood that neurons will fire; and (3) transform the 'shape' of a neuron's spiking or bursting activity (Brezina 2010). Consider Eve Marder's (2012) groundbreaking work on a bundle of approximately thirty neurons (the stomatogastric ganglion) that regulate the activity of crustacean stomach muscles. A diverse range of chemical signals are employed to adjust the frequency of spiking, the number of spikes per burst, and the phase relationships between different cells within this network to yield different patterns of activity. A single circuit can be modulated in different ways by serotonin, dopamine, and octopamine. Moreover, a single chemical signal like dopamine can modulate the currents through a single cell in multiple different ways by binding to different locations on a cell, and it can modulate activity differently in different neurons. By boosting or suppressing activity in specific circuits, and filtering specific kinds of information, chemical processes shape experience across changing contexts. Consequently, it will sometimes be useful to interpret neural processes as analog computations that rely upon medium-dependent representations. Where this is true, we will need to understand the physical properties of the neural system if we are to understand how it does what it does (Maley 2021, 14745); this means that it will often be more productive to focus on the ways that neural activity is constrained by chemical signals that orient animals directly toward ecologically and socially salient information.

From this perspective, we might therefore say that while neural activity is essential to the ongoing regulation of thought and behavior, it is often shaped by chemical signaling systems that convey physiological demands from distributed bodily systems. These demands must be satisfied for the body to cope with challenges and opportunities. Moreover, in many cases, widely distributed networks of neural and bodily processes will need to be integrated to sustain active engagement with ecologically and socially relevant phenomena. In this context, appeals to functional localization and decomposition, and to claims about the computational processes that are employed by a system, should not be taken for granted. On the one hand, although chemical signals are often produced locally, within a specific neural network, they can also be produced in distant parts of the brain or in distant bodily locations; but in every case, they will shape activity across a wide range of bodily and neural systems, ranging from various peripheral organs – including the gastrointestinal tract, heart, kidneys – to diverse cortical and subcortical neural networks.

This situation is further complicated by three significant features of the brain. First, the processes that must be integrated to preserve viability will often be distributed across the brain, body, and world, and a diverse range of strategies will need to be employed, often in parallel, to manage numerous social and ecological challenges. Second, neural activity often unfolds across multiple temporal scales. Some processes are regulated by local patterns of neural spiking and rapidly dissipating chemical signals; others depend upon more robust chemical signals that affect embodied activity over longer timescales (for example, serotonin and dopamine). Finally, and perhaps most importantly, brains are heterarchical systems (see Section 1.4) that employ networks of distributed, flexibly coupled, interacting processes that collectively create and manipulate the diverse sources of information that are necessary to preserve viability in changing environments.

With regard to the first two claims, biological processes will often be specialized for processing certain kinds of information. But this does not entail that processing should be understood as modular, in the sense that localized components will correspond to meaningful psychological categories (such as attention, language, or social cognition). There are a couple of reasons for this. First, the chemical signals that are employed to regulate the flow of information throughout the brain and body can be used in different ways, by different systems, in different contexts. Second, neural processes are often reused and integrated into different networks, as animals cope with diverse challenges and opportunities. In both cases, the guiding hypothesis should be that "resource constraints and efficiency considerations dictate that whenever possible neural, behavioral, and environmental resources [will be] reused and redeployed in support of any newly emerging cognitive capacities" (Anderson 2014, 7). Against this backdrop, it is worth saying a bit more about the heterarchical organization of the brain, given that this suggestion is likely to be unfamiliar to many readers.

It is perhaps easiest to conceptualize heterarchical control in political domains, where it is clear what it would mean to say that there is no central controller and no 'top' to the system. This doesn't mean that the political domain lacks organization. But the interactions between different parts of a heterarchical society can change, in ways that are sensitive to the needs of the broader system of social organization, and the management of different kinds of challenges can lead a heterarchical society to exploit different kinds of control structures, in different contexts. For example, the management of long-range trade agreements might exploit higher-order control structures, while communal interactions and local manufacturing might be organized by neighborhood or shop. But things get interesting when trade-offs must be negotiated between these different social processes. In a heterarchical society, such trade-offs must be carried out flexibly and dynamically, without any top-level system to regulate them. Sometimes coordination will unfold at lower levels of aggregation, and sometimes higher-level patterns of cooperation will arise, with collective interactions serving to regulate the interactions that occur at the lower level. Finally, strategies that are accepted in the short run can become deeply entrenched if they are not challenged. But the key thing to note is that the observed patterns of organization should not be assumed to exist necessarily: they are structures of control that were established for specific purposes, and many of them can change in response to different demands, often by reorganizing the interactions between multiple control systems.

In the context of cognitive and neural architecture, many kinds of processes and constraints, operating across numerous different timescales and numerous patterns of interaction, must be organized to preserve viability in the face of diverse challenges. Sometimes, this will allow for the use of high-level process-ing to make plans or to manage different trade-offs; sometimes it will require managing multiple trade-offs in parallel, at a much lower level of aggregation in the absence of centralized control; and in many cases strategies for managing diverse challenges will come to reflect an animal's history, as well as the contextual factors that are relevant to the preservation of viability. The claim that brains are heterarchical systems, then, entails that many parallel lines of organization operate across many different timescales and structures of inter-action to guide thought and behavior.

Many physiological and social demands are managed by chemical signals that are directly related to a specific state (for example, low plasma sodium or changes in blood glucose) or by chemical signals that carry information about specific physiological demands (Herbert & Schulkin 2002, 661). In these contexts, decentralized interactions between various processes can sustain the continuous evaluation of bodily and cognitive processes, and they can do so across variations in resource availability, fluctuations in the risk of pursuing a resource, the changing cost of energy expenditure, and differences in the likelihood of success. Stable regulatory strategies will tend to emerge as diverse processes become attuned to reliably present resources or reliably present demands; however, even in these contexts, interactions among distributed processes can often be employed beyond this first pass at prioritizing and responding to the biological and social demands that organize biological cognition.

Long-range chemical signals also shape neural activity, as well as the activity of peripheral organs (including the gastrointestinal tract, heart, kidneys, and more). This is where more complex forms of control begin to come into play. These chemical processes recruit cortical and subcortical networks that are relevant to managing specific physiological demands, and they induce changes in the peripheral bodily systems that must be prepared to cope with various kinds of social and physiological challenges and opportunities. Collectively, these processes organize behavior across changes in the internal, ecological, and social milieu, and they do so without requiring centralized control, as many of these processes have evolved to monitor and respond to specific changes in the internal or external milieu, using low-cost appraisal systems that operate continuously (Schulkin & Sterling 2019). By regulating the flow of different chemical signals (such as oxytocin, angiotensin, dopamine, norepinephrine, corticotropin-releasing hormone, and more), these processes sustain the integration of salient information about bodily and cognitive states across distributed information-processing systems, and they do so in ways that motivate behavior, specify priority relations, and sustain predictions regarding the efficacy of responding or failing to respond in the current ecological and social context.

Summarizing, we claim that biological cognition exploits heterarchical networks of analog and digital processes that are continually adjusted to preserve predictive coherence across various domains of cognitive and social life. We also claim that many chemical and neural networks are tightly coupled to specific changes in biological variables (including the need for glucose, oxygen, sodium, social comfort, and more), and we contend that in these cases divergences between anticipated and actual states will evoke experiences that alert animals to the behaviors that must be taken to preserve viability. That said, there are other processes that are less tightly coupled to immediate physiological and social needs, so it is sometimes necessary to employ anticipations or representations to cope with available challenges and opportunities. But even where representations are employed, as they are in domains like syntactic and morphological processing, there will be multiple pathways toward stabilizing the relevant forms of thought and experience, and the necessity of managing different challenges will produce different kinds of processing strategies to achieve broadly similar ends (we return to this point in the final section of this Element).

This last point is key! Explaining how diverse processes establish coherent and stable forms of thought and experience often requires acknowledging that adjustments can occur in numerous locations, yielding effects that stretch beyond the domain where they initially occurred (Rosen & Schulkin 2004). Moreover, when one element is imprecise or noisy, other processes will often be mobilized or adjusted to achieve coherence, even where the point of stability that is achieved diverges radically from more typical forms of cognition (Corlett et al. 2019). This raises serious questions about how large-scale integration can occur within a heterarchical network of neural processes. To get a sense of what integration amounts to, it will help to consider an analogy to an audio mixing console in a recording studio (Figure 2).

1.4 Integration in Heterarchical Networks

A mixing console receives numerous kinds of structured input, and it uses various analog and digital processes to create a unified and distinctive tone. In such a system, multiple variables must often be adjusted in parallel, and the output of such a system will always be sensitive to the structure of the current inputs and the settings on numerous different processing parameters. The weighting of different inputs can be adjusted, and parameters can be weighted differently in different contexts. That said, changes in one set of parameters will often need to be compensated for by changes in others, and in every case the producer must attempt to achieve a coherent and stable output by weighting

Figure 2 An audio mixing console.
Public domain image. Studio One, Windmill Lane Studios, Dublin. Wikimedia Commons

different flows of information in accordance with the aesthetic demands of a particular musical style. There are many ways to achieve something aesthetic-ally pleasing, and there will often be many ways to achieve a similar sound. But, just as importantly, the weightings within a mixing board can yield patterns of path dependency that make it difficult to achieve aesthetic coherence without adjusting numerous other levels in the system.

Cognition operates in a similar way, by integrating different processes and adjusting different levels on processing parameters. There is no single way to set the parameters, and different needs or different challenges can lead to different but nonetheless coherent settings. In a wide range of contexts, such as eating, reproducing, regulating circadian rhythms, and integrating sensori-motor information, chemical signals are employed to adjust the strength of neural connections, to modulate neural firing rates, and to convey information from diverse bodily locations – often in the form of regulatory demands (Marder 2012). This often yields forms of adaptive regulation that are tightly coupled to ecological considerations, including the location and value of resources, and the time of day or the time of the year when resources are likely to be available. But learning and development also shape the strategies an animal will employ to navigate physiological and social challenges and opportunities. In complex and unpredictable environments, however, the preservation of viability is not a panacea. Instead of sustaining optimal performance, biological processes aim at 'good enough' solutions to the challenges that arise – and sometimes the available solutions are not good enough to sustain flourishing or even survival. Furthermore, sustained patterns of need and stress can shift the ways that animals respond to various bodily and social needs, modulating complex cascades of physiological processes across diverse biological systems and making it difficult to change habitual behaviors in ways that can bring about a more positive state (Sterling & Eyer 1988).

Fortunately, cognition is also flexible, and it exploits a multidimensional search for plausible ways of navigating challenges and opportunities. Unlike the adjustments on a mixing console, which are made by a person, cognition must employ decentralized networks of neural and chemical processes to adjust the levels on various processes. This is where the appeal to heterarchical organization really pays off. Experience and behavior are shaped by diverse neural and chemical processes that collectively direct animals to engage in actions that will (hopefully) preserve viability through change. Critically, many physiological and social demands recruit actions directly, to satisfy specific needs, trigger specific regulatory strategies, or evoke cascades of changes across bodily and neural systems that yield global shifts in physiological regulation and cognition. These processes are not centrally controlled, and each of them conveys distinctive demands, which can be monitored, amplified, manipulated, or even ignored by subsequent processing.

Where additional processing resources are required to navigate a challenge or opportunity, chemical signals are used to shift the integration of perceptual and bodily inputs with stored information. Sometimes this will open space for more reflective thought and analysis (Shine et al. 2022), but it can also produce atypical and divergent forms of experience and reasoning. For example, traumatic and nontraumatic forms of voice-hearing appear to reflect changes in the weighting of past experience, relative to current sensory input (Powers et al. 2017). These compensatory responses can buffer against persisting difficulties, but they can also yield the differential effects of hallucinations and delusions. Likewise, psilocybin, cannabinoids, ketamine, and dopamine agonists all appear to alter perception and cognition by enhancing or diminishing the role of expectations relative to perceptual inputs (Corlett et al. 2009). Finally, the differences between hallucinations and delusions may reflect adjustments to different chemically regulated processes that lead expectations to be assigned more weight in one part of a cognitive system and less weight in another part of that same system (the precise nature of these effects is still unclear, but see Sterzer et al. 2018 for a plausible attempt to situate these claims within a computational model of psychosis). From a computational perspective, it seems likely that these effects will be best explained by appeal to hierarchical models – and it is worth considering this possibility in detail.

1.5 Is Cognition Governed by a Hierarchical Model?

Suppose you expect a cup to be filled with a warm, slightly bitter liquid that tastes chocolatey, with hints of pomegranate and sugar cane. If this cup of coffee is cold, sour, or ashy, you will update your model and shift your behavior accordingly (perhaps you will hold your nose and drink it, or perhaps you will pour it down the drain). Such phenomena have led many researchers to hypothesize that brains construct models of the world that represent the likely causes of sensory and interoceptive events, as well as the latent variables that support accurate predictions and effective actions (Seth & Tsakiris 2018).

A broadly Bayesian explanation of these patterns of thought and behavior would appeal to: (1) a model of what coffee should taste like; (2) error signals that arise in response to mismatches between expected and actual outcomes; and (3) algorithms for using error signals to improve a model of what coffee can be like, or to motivate activity that brings the world into alignment with your model of what coffee must be. This is an instance of a general learning strategy. When there are differences between expected and actual states, error signals can be produced. As these error signals flow 'upward' through a computational hierarchy, they can trigger adjustments to settings at higher levels, bringing higher-level expectations into alignment with observed states, and this can lead to the recruitment of new actions as well as new expectations. At the same time, expectations flow 'downward' through that hierarchy, resolving ambiguities in the incoming data and imposing additional structure in accordance with the brain's best guess about what makes the incoming data meaningful. Over time, this bidirectional flow of information is thought to support the construction of accurate and useful models of the world, as it shows up from the brain's point of view.

From the perspective that this approach to cognition inspires, animals experience their brain's best guess about the likely causes of its current state. Put somewhat differently, animals do not passively receive information from the world, nor do they experience the world directly in an unmediated way. Instead, they are thought to actively construct experience using predictive algorithms that rely on information acquired through previous actions to generate a best guess about what is likely to happen; likewise, their patterns of thought and perception are understood as forms of anticipatory inference that reflect the flow of information through a brain that is trying to minimize the differences between its expectations and its perceptual inputs. This yields a simple and unified approach to cognition, where the brain can be understood as a central processing unit that decodes the data it receives, using simple rules for manipulating, transforming, and storing information.

Theorists who adopt a Bayesian approach to cognition often claim that sparse data from sensory and bodily systems are insufficient to specify the features of the world we encounter. Thought and experience unfold in a world of alarm calls, meaningful sentences, musical genres, complex flavor profiles, and immersive experiences of horror films or period dramas. But the cochlea only responds to patterned sound waves, the olfactory epithelium only responds to chemical compounds, and photons are the only thing that hits the retina. Therefore, it is proposed that the brain must construct a causal model of the world to fill in gaps, smooth out noise, and assign meaning to ambiguous signals (Tenenbaum et al. 2011). This can be done using a simple form of Bayesian inference, where a model of the world is adjusted when it fails to represent salient aspects of the world. Setting the parameters of this model in different ways can yield the kinds of effects that we have just discussed.

There are serious limitations to this approach, some of which we explore throughout this Element. To begin with, this approach treats the brain as a unified control system that is contingently embedded within a body that contingently inhabits a world. But animals are embodied beings, with evolutionary and developmental histories that have produced capacities for managing the social and ecological challenges that are relevant to survival and flourishing (Corris 2020). As we learn more about these constraints, it becomes clear that many perceptual and physiological processes are sufficient to guide thought and behavior without further construction (Anderson & Chemero 2019, 166). This is not to deny that interesting things happen when sound waves hit the cochlea, when chemical compounds hit the olfactory epithelium, or when photons hit the retina. In each of these cases, chemical and bioelectrical activity cascades through complex networks of neural systems, shaping thought and experience. But to understand how thought and experience are shaped by chemical signals and neural activity, theoretical and empirical tools must be used that are rarely employed in computational and representational accounts of cognition.

To get a sense of what this means, it will help to turn to an alternative story that is more tightly coupled to the physiology of perceptual systems. At the very least, this will yield a supplement to the Bayesian approach that many philosophers and cognitive scientists are currently exploring – but it might also require an even more radical revision to the way that we approach biological cognition. In any case, it will lead us to think differently about what it means to see things that matter.

2 Seeing Things That Matter

Animals must track threats and dangers, respond to them where necessary, and develop strategies for avoiding adversity where possible. This requires perceiving the world around them in terms that highlight things that matter to survival and flourishing. For many animals, this means that diverse capacities are employed in parallel to track predators, while also responding to the level of threat that specific predators pose. For example, since humans are often the most salient predator for free-roaming elephants, they learn to track the visual and olfactory cues that are associated with different groups of people; at the same time, they become sensitive to acoustic phenomena that are associated with risk, including subtle vocal signals of age, gender, and ethnicity (McComb et al. 2014).

Each sensory system employs its own strategies to organize ecologically meaningful information. Auditory systems detect, extract, segregate, and group acoustic regularities into stable perceptual units (Bizley & Cohen 2013, 693), and they do so in ways that are sensitive to the fact that sounds are typically unavailable for reexamination or further processing after they have occurred. By contrast, olfaction exploits a form of combinatorial coding and receptor tuning that makes it possible to track minimal variations in chemical composition without context-invariant representations (Barwich 2019). These sources of sensory information are continually integrated into the experience of an animal who is attempting to survive and flourish in a dangerous and often unpredictable world, and they are constantly modulated by a diverse array of appraisal systems that are distributed throughout the brainstem, midbrain, and cortex (Schulkin et al. 2003).

In the context of typical human experience, vision often takes precedence over the other senses (Stokes et al. 2015); moreover, research on vision often takes precedence over research into the other senses. Consequently, a great deal is known about how chemical and neural processes are integrated by visual systems, so in this section our aim is to show that attending to these processes can clarify the limitations of simple and unified approaches to cognition, especially when such approaches rely on functional decomposition and unsubstantiated claims about digital computations.

2.1 Early Gestures toward a Constructive Theory of Vision

In the early days of the cognitive sciences, researchers commonly drew upon insights from physiology, ethology, and artificial intelligence to develop hypotheses about how animals track and respond to meaningful information. One intriguing hypothesis derived from the discovery of ganglion cells in frogs' retinae that responded selectively to edges, curvature, motion, and contrast. Jerome Lettvin and colleagues (1959) hypothesized that these cells supported parallel information channels that were manipulated by cells in the optic tectum to drive food-finding and predator-evasion, in bright as well as dim environments. They couldn't specify precisely which operations were carried out, but they speculated that perceptions of ecologically significant phenomena were *constructed*, and they gestured toward Oliver Selfridge's (1959) work with pattern recognizers like *Pandemonium*. *Pandemonium* was a feed-forward network that categorized patterns using three kinds of 'demons': (1) processing units that responded by 'screaming' when they encountered their preferred stimuli; (2) processing units that monitored these 'screams' and adjusted their own 'screams' as a function of the convergence between what they 'expected' and what they 'observed'; and (3) a processing unit that selected the 'loudest' scream as the system's output.

The idea that neurons were organized into columns that could implement a feed-forward architecture like this was consistent with existing knowledge of physiology. By the late nineteenth century, Santiago Ramón y Cajal (1899) had discovered that sensory neurons have a relatively orderly and directed pattern of organization (Figure 3), and in the late 1950s, David Hubel and Torsten Wiesel (1959, 1962) discovered feature detectors in cats' primary visual cortices that responded to light and dark lines, with specific orientations, in specific locations in the visual field. Like Lettvin and his colleagues, they hypothesized that information from 'simple cells' served as input to 'complex cells,' which sent information to 'hypercomplex cells.' This would allow increasingly abstract properties to be processed as information flowed through networks of cells with similar receptive fields, and because adjacent columns appeared to process adjacent sources of information, these structures could produce a map of the visually perceptible environment. Data collected in other labs provided additional support for the claim that "neurophysiology and sensation are best linked by looking at the flow of information rather than simpler measures of neuronal activity" (Barlow 1972, 376). By the mid-1970s, many researchers held that retinal information was progressively transformed into a sensitivity to shape and orientation as successive operations were carried out in the visual cortex (Wurtz 2009, 2819).

This story was complicated, however, by data suggesting that even stationary visual systems manage the flow of information by selectively removing irrelevant patterns of contrast and spatial frequency. Numerous experiments demonstrated a reduced sensitivity to *similar* patterns of spatial frequency and orientation after an animal fixated on a target, and it was suggested that such effects revealed patterns of processing fatigue in orientation-specific and

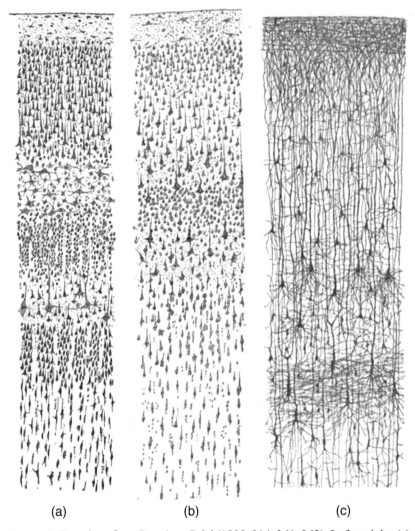

(a)   (b)   (c)

Figure 3 Drawings from Ramón y Cajal (1899, 314, 361, 363). Left to right: (a) visual cortex of a human adult. (b) motor cortex of a human adult. (c) cortex of a one-and-a-half-month-old infant.

Public domain image, *Cajal cortex drawings* (author: Looie496), Wikimedia commons.

frequency-specific cells (Blakemore & Campbell 1969). Such effects were anchored to the receptive fields of cells in the visual cortex, which typically have either an on-center/off-surround arrangement or an off-center/on-surround arrange-ment. That is, the activity of these cells either increased when bright stimuli were presented in a specific location while being inhibited by bright stimuli in surround-ing regions or vice versa; moreover, bright stimuli that covered both the specific location and surrounding regions would yield little or no response, yielding a phenomenon known as lateral inhibition. It seemed likely that examining the collective activity of these cells would make it possible to track all of the patterns of visual information without any appeal to action, and it was hypothesized that interactions within these networks could sustain a sensitivity to the geometric features of the world (Campbell & Maffei 1974, 106). From this perspective, it began to seem like the neural code could be understood directly, without ever appealing to the contingent needs or interests of an animal.

Against this backdrop, David Marr (1982) articulated a *computational* approach to vision as a way of integrating mathematical models with behavioral and neurophysiological data. Marr had done important work on retinal filtering, binocular vision, and object recognition. But he felt that these physiological approaches were insufficient to explain *why* animals experience the things they do. For example, he acknowledged that spatial filters played a significant role in vision, but he argued that understanding how an animal represents the geometric structure of the world, and makes this geometric information available for further processing, required an account of the algorithms that are used to process this information. Likewise, he claimed that even if feature detection occurs, an algorithmic approach would be necessary to explain why a frog represents flies, as opposed to small, moving, black spots of about the right size.

The key thing to notice is that Marr began from the assumption that retinal data are always noisy and sparse. This led him to propose that the information in a retinal image must be manipulated and transformed to produce a useful description that is not cluttered with irrelevant information. He drew upon existing models of edge detection, the minimization of the angular discrepancy between retinal images, and the ability to compute shape from texture, contour, and shading, and he proposed that visual processing is a multistage constructive process. Put much too simply, he claimed that variations in spatial geometry, reflectance properties, illumination, and viewpoint – which are often muddled in naturalistic scenes – are detected and integrated into a 'raw primal sketch'; detail is then progressively added to construct representations of visual geometry, including representations of depth and spatial organization.

Importantly, Marr (1982, 331) advised against following a specific recipe for developing an approach to vision, noting that important insights into the nature of visual processing could come from neurology, neuroscience, behavioral science, or even phenomenology. But at the same time, he proposed that vision science should always begin from the articulation of a precise *computational description* of what vision does and why. Such descriptions proceed at a high level of generality, and they are neither process models nor specifications of the algorithms employed to solve specific tasks. They delimit the space of *algorithmic explanations* that must be considered in figuring out how a visual system might solve the computational problem that it faces. In clarifying the class of rule-governed transformations that might be used by a visual system, algorithmic explanations must abstract away from the complexities of biological systems; but by employing representational strategies, they aim to characterize the meaningful features of the information that must be processed. Finally, Marr proposed that algorithmic explanations could bridge the gap between behavior and neural processing, but doing so required an account of how the algorithms that *could* be used to solve specific tasks are *implemented* (in a brain, circuit board, or virtual environment). Critically, it was only at this point that it became necessary to explain how the parts of a biological system are organized and how they change.

Versions of this approach have dominated much recent theorizing about perception. But this approach raises numerous questions. Is the retinal image really noisy and sparse? Must a constructive process be used to introduce the details that are present in a visual experience but absent in the retinal signal? Do brains really employ algorithmic processes to extract useable and meaningful information from meaningless data? We take the answers to these questions to be far from obvious. Therefore, in the remainder of this section, we argue that the primary role of visual systems is to orient animals toward those sources of information that are relevant to their survival and their potential for flourishing. We have no doubt that this requires numerous forms of information processing, but we are skeptical of the claim that detail must be progressively added to simple visual percepts, creating meaning on the basis of meaningless data. For this reason, we think that it is worth considering Marr's (1982, 29–31) surprising claim that J. J. Gibson comes closest to providing an alternative to his computational description of what vision does, and why.

2.2 A More Biological Approach to Vision

According to Gibson, the constructivism that has dominated research on vision is an artifact of using simplified experiments that force animals to cope with minimal stimuli and snapshots of scenes that are flashed at them briefly. In ecologically valid contexts, animals often move around and examine things from multiple different perspectives to resolve perceptual ambiguities. Gibson argued that these behavioral strategies are as much a part of perceiving as anything that happens in the eye (or any part of the brain), and he proposed that *animals* should be understood as possessing the skills they need for tracking perceptual invariants, or features of the world that are stable across changes, including changes driven by their *activities* (Gibson 1979).

From this perspective, it is a mistake to assume that brains construct perceptual experiences by sifting through and integrating noisy data. Instead, Gibson claims that perception brings animals into contact with aspects of the world that matter, revealing the possibilities for action that the world affords. He also resists appeals to information processing and suggests that perception is more like tuning an analog radio to pick up a specific signal. Some readers of this Element may be unfamiliar with the radios that Gibson was imagining, so it is worth clarifying three key features of this analogy:

1. Tuning a radio is a process that isolates a sine wave, using patterns of internal *resonance* to amplify one waveform while limiting interference from others.
2. To the extent that a signal can be heard on a radio, this involves the entire system – removing any of its inner workings will compromise the ability to isolate the signal, and it will be impossible to decompose the system into separate pieces that represent different parts of the waveforms, even though each component plays specific roles in the overall functioning of the radio.
3. Tuning such a radio can sometimes necessitate moving the entire radio around in order to find a signal that can be amplified and isolated.

From the perspective of this analogy, perception is an active process that depends on numerous interacting capacities for tracking the possibilities the world affords.

Drawing inspiration from this approach, Roger Shepard (1984) proposed a way of integrating Gibson's framework with insights from neuroscience. He claimed that under "favorable conditions of illumination, mobility, and so on, our experience of the environment is so tightly guided by the externally available information that we readily feel the appropriateness of Gibson's term *direct perception*" (Shepard 1984, 422). But he agrees with Marr that information processing is likely to be necessary in some contexts, given the complexity of the visual system, the roles of visual information in imagination, thinking, and dreaming, and the perturbation of vision by drugs and disease. Shepard does not, however, appeal to progressive and constructive computations; instead, he argues that such experiences reflect the internalization of processing constraints, which facilitate forms of behavior that are more flexible and less bound up with immediate patterns of stimulation. Since the notion of processing constraints is likely to be unfamiliar to some readers of this Element, it is worth exploring this suggestion in more detail.

In clarifying his claims about processing constraints, Shepard offers an analogy to circadian rhythms. It was initially assumed that circadian rhythms are directly regulated by exposure to sunlight, since all organisms – from cyanobacteria to humans – synchronize biological variables in response to light–dark cycles. Intriguingly, circadian rhythms will often deviate from a twenty-four-hour cycle by a few minutes per day in the absence of exposure to predicted light–dark cycles; however, a brief exposure to sunlight at a predicted time will re-entrain these rhythms. These patterns of wandering and recalibration suggest that the periodicity of circadian rhythms has been *internalized*, to sustain the regulation of the internal milieu without reliable external stimulation, and we might therefore say that internalized rhythms *constrain* the ability of complex organisms to entrain to predictable light–dark cycles. This makes sense, as a diurnal animal must regulate their internal milieu even if they are forced to stay in a dark burrow to avoid predation, and they must be able to use whatever visual cues happen to be available to synchronize patterns of internal regulation (Shepard 1984, 422).

According to Shepard, when external phenomena are stable across evolutionary timescales, they will tend to be internalized as processing constraints that structure and organize cognition. For example, he claims that visual processing is shaped by geometric constraints that organize visual information in accordance with stable relations of perspective, predictable patterns in moving bodies, and the likelihood that light comes from above.

> When stimulated by a strong natural signal, as under favorable conditions of motion and illumination, the system's resonant coupling with the world would be tight enough to give rise to what Gibson called *direct perception*. However, the coupling is tight only because an appropriate match has evolved between the externally available information and the internalized constraints. (Shepard 1984, 433)

We might not recognize the operation of geometric constraints when the resonant coupling is tight. But Shepard claims that internalized geometric constraints operate where typical sources of perceptual input are absent, and he argues that even in the best cases, perception will always reflect interactions between invariant features of the world and invariant structures that have shaped perceptual systems over the course of evolutionary timescales (Shepard 1984, 421).

We find this approach plausible. But it must be supplemented by a more robust account of the physiological constraints that regulate the flow of information through the visual system, given the wide range of biological and social challenges that can compromise the tight coupling between an animal and their world. For example, predators and prey must be tracked in dense fogs and low-lighting conditions, and they must be identified when glimpsed briefly and when they are partially obscured. In such contexts, a biologically plausible visual system should be able to exploit physiological processes that enhance or suppress available sources of information. Likewise, it must be possible for physiological constraints to produce visual experiences with minimal connections to external information – in dreams, and in the context of sensory deprivation or visual deficits. From our perspective, *ecological constraints* shape perceptual systems and *physiological constraints* organize the flow of information through perceptual systems, and this is true even though biological perception is a process that is continually shaped by opportunities for action.

One promising way of developing this proposal has recently been advanced by György Buzsáki (2019). He contends that perceiving things that matter requires calibrating endogenous neural activity through action. While his proposal is somewhat speculative, the claim that spontaneous neural activity biases perception is well supported (Engel et al. 2001). For our purposes, however, the key thing to notice is that Buzsáki (2019) acknowledges that 'preconfigured' constraints shape the actions and perceptions that will be possible for an animal. He is open to the possibility that external constraints that are stable across evolutionary timescales are internalized as processing constraints, and he argues that the calibration of endogenous neural activity allows animals to perceive things as meaningful and to simulate things in the absence of perceptual input or action. Preserving Gibson's insight that perception is an active process requires thinking about the diverse set of information-processing capacities that sustain perceptual constancy across changes in perspective, orientation, and motion. As we argue in the remainder of this section, a wide range of neural systems are employed to enhance and suppress aspects of the incoming signal, in ways that are sensitive to constraints on energy and efficiency, as well as constraints imposed by motor demands and the necessity of regulating the internal milieu (Sterling & Laughlin 2015).

Before exploring this claim in physiological detail, it will help to consider an analogy that is close to Gibson's appeal to tuning a radio: the stimulation of sensory receptors is transformed into an experience of a world using a network of process that are analogous to analog and digital effects, which transform the vibrations of plucked guitar strings into more complex sound patterns (Figure 4). When a guitar string is plucked above an electromagnetic pickup, its vibrations are converted into an electrical current with variable voltage. The simplest transformations take the form of *amplification*, generating a stronger voltage to drive the vibrations in a loudspeaker, as electrical energy is transformed into mechanical energy using a second electromagnetic system. But differently textured sounds can be produced by transforming the waveform that reaches the loudspeaker, and signals can be manipulated to eliminate noise, enhance features of the source signal, or create novel patterns by transforming specific aspects of

Figure 4 A guitar connected to a complex network of analog and digital pedals.
Photo courtesy of Daniel Wyche.

the source signal. Some effects modulate the frequency of a signal, while others
compensate for variations in the signal by enhancing or suppressing the amplitude
of the waveform, and more complex effects can be applied to different aspects of
the signal (for example, the attack or delay), boosting, suppressing, or clipping
them to change the shape of the resulting waveform. Finally, parts of a signal can
be separated, processed independently, and reintegrated, or integrated with
internal oscillators, to generate the distinctive patterns that are indicative of
different acoustic forms.

It would be easy to misread this analogy from a Cartesian point of view. But
there is no one who listens to the music, and there is no one sitting in a Cartesian
theater. Like Gibson, we contend that perception is a matter of getting a grip on

the aspects of the world that matter, and this requires sensitivities to worldly sources of information. Unlike Gibson, we hold that this information can be manipulated to produce a wider range of behavioral and cognitive effects. More precisely, we hold that perceptual experience relies upon numerous forms of signal manipulation (including boosting, suppression, filtering, separation, and reintegration) to sustain the stability of visual experience across diverse attempts to respond to challenges and opportunities. But this is not a matter of creating a representation; it is a way of shaping capacities to respond to available sources of information. So when we claim that vision manipulates diverse sources of information, over multiple timescales, we are making a claim about how a perceiving animal manages the stable, transient, and context-sensitive features of the world where they need to live and act.

Sometimes, the analog computations that are employed to process information are directly reflected in biological processes. Sometimes, the transformation of visual information requires complex and distributed forms of information processing, making it less clear how these processes are implemented, even where behavioral data provide clear evidence of signal manipulation. But in every case, perceptual processes should be understood as tracking and responding to the significant challenges that an animal must face. Ecological psychologists are likely to be unhappy with the role of information processing in this story, but we contend that this is the most plausible way of integrating insights from computational neuroscience with research on the physiology of visual systems and with Gibson's claim that vision is an activity that unfolds as animals explore their world.

2.3 Early Vision

It would be impossible to provide a complete biological account of vision in this Element. Indeed, it would take an entire Element just to explain the patterns of information processing that occur in the retina, where numerous forms of linear filtering and gain control are employed to stabilize visual experience (see Box 1). Consequently, we shall only highlight some of the interacting processes that support capacities for tracking and responding to the information that matters to an animal that must face numerous predictable and unpredictable challenges.

There is a highly conserved visual processing pathway that leads from the retina to the superior colliculus (the optic tectum in nonmammalian vertebrates), a multilayered network that sits atop the brainstem. Across species, networks centering on the superior colliculus facilitate the ongoing integration of visual information with auditory, vestibular, and proprioceptive

Box 1 Visual Signal Manipulation Begins in the Eye

The organization and structure of the retina can be taken as a small-scale model of the account of the visual system that we develop in this section. Retinal cells are organized into three distinct layers:

1. **A layer of** *photoreceptors*, including *rods*, which respond in low-lighting conditions, and up to five different types of *cones*, which respond to different frequencies of brighter light. There is also a small class of photosensitive cells that entrain circadian rhythms, but most retinal cells process the information detected by photoreceptors.
2. **An intermediate layer**, which includes *horizontal cells* that increase contrast via lateral inhibition, facilitating adaptation to both brighter and dimmer light conditions; eleven types of *bipolar cells*, which transfer information from photoreceptors to ganglion cells, using simple forms of signal boosting and signal suppression; and between twenty-two and thirty types of *amacrine cells*, which rely on chemical signals – including acetylcholine, dopamine, gamma-aminobutyric acid (GABA), and glycine – to modulate the flow of information through the retina.
3. **A layer of** *retinal ganglion cells*, which controls the flow of information to the rest of the brain.

Collectively, these physiological structures sustain a sensitivity to spatial information and motion. They also facilitate forms of temporal filtering, spatial averaging, signal boosting, signal suppression, and signal integration that reduce the amount of information that must be processed downstream, and they rapidly discard the aspects of the signal that are unlikely to be informative given an animal's needs and interests (Baden et al. 2020). Many of these processes are shared across species, but the different challenges that different animals must face lead to variations in the distribution and number of retinal cells – across species and within species – which reflect everything from energy limitations to differences in body temperature to differences in the statistics of the local environment.

In a human eye, for example, retinal cells must use the information that is present as light drifts across the eye to reduce $\sim 10^7$ events at the photoreceptors to a single spike in a ganglion cell over the course of ~ 100 ms. This makes it clear that the light hitting the retina is not an impoverished source of information; instead, there is too much information for a brain to use – and this yields a distinctive problem for the visual system. Given the energetic cost of spiking, and the recovery time required after a burst of neuronal activity, a mean spiking rate ~100 times faster than anything that is observed in the brain would be necessary for the eye to carry out this task (Sterling & Laughlin 2015, 277). So instead, analog and chemical processes are employed to filter, transform, and prioritize different sources of information. Directionally sensitive cells, for example, support a kind of analog signal delay, which makes it possible to rapidly extract motion information (Mauss et al. 2017), and starburst amacrine cells exploit GABA and acetylcholine to modulate the intensity of incoming signals and increase the reliability of information about light moving across the retina (Anderson 2015). By relying upon diverse forms of parallel signal processing, across multiple timescales, the retinal signal preserves the stability of perceptual experience across continuous changes in sensory information (Baccus & Meister 2002), but this is also the reason why stabilizing the retinal image will often lead visual experience to disappear in as little as ~100 ms.

information (see Figures 5 and 6). While these networks may not sustain the rich phenomenology that is commonly associated with visual experience, they clearly support the rapid orientation toward targets, threats, and other salient phenomena. In frogs and toads, these networks support rapid sensorimotor responses to predators and prey (Ewert 1984, 1997). In barn owls, they are employed to calibrate visual and auditory processing, allowing for rapid prey detection and capture in typical perceptual contexts – but just as importantly, they also sustain the capacity to adapt to visual distortions induced by prism goggles (Hyde & Knudsen 2002). Finally, in primates, these networks regulate eye gaze and head direction in response to cortically driven shifts in attention (Goldberg & Wurtz 1972); they also sustain sensitivities to location and orientation in the context of human blindsight (Tamietto et al. 2010), and a pathway linking the superior colliculus to the thalamus and amygdala regulates threat detection and affect, with atypical activity in this system yielding behavioral sensitivities that look a lot like posttraumatic stress disorder (Wang et al. 2020). In each of these contexts, the key thing to notice is that the superior colliculus preserves the spatial organization of sensory information and modulates action selection and perceptual orientation using various neurotransmitters to boost the salience of specific stimuli and specific responses (Krauzlis et al. 2013).

In many mammals, a second visual processing pathway leads from the retina to the thalamus – a bundle of nuclei just above the brainstem. Specifically, this

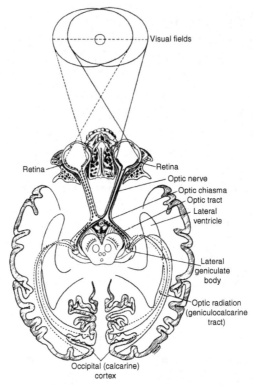

Figure 5 An anatomical depiction of the retinogeniculate pathway, leading from the retina to the lateral geniculate nucleus and primary visual cortex (including V1) in the occipital lobe.
From House and Pansky (1960). Public domain image.

pathway leads to a multilayered network known as the lateral geniculate nucleus. Like the superior colliculus, the lateral geniculate nucleus preserves the spatial organization of sensory information, but its activity highlights the geometric features of the world, organizing information to preserve the tight connection between animals and the spatial organization of their environments. Different layers of the lateral geniculate nucleus sustain forms of luminance gain control, contrast gain control, and temporal weighting, which normalize inputs from the retina and minimize the impact of sudden changes in luminance and contrast (Carandini et al. 2005, 10581). These processes are context sensitive, and ongoing feedback from the cortex sustains continuous adjustments in response to changes in visual contrast, stimulus size, and background luminance; moreover, activity in the lateral geniculate nucleus is shaped by a diverse array of chemical signals (including acetylcholine, $GABA_A$, $GABA_B$, and

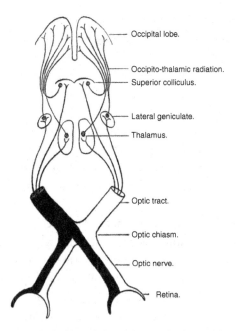

Figure 6 A schematic depiction of the retinogeniculate pathway, leading from the retina to the lateral geniculate nucleus and primary visual cortex (including V1) in the occipital lobe, which also highlights the retinotectal pathway that leads from the retina to the superior colliculus and primary visual cortex (including V1) in the occipital lobe.
Adapted from Howell (1916). Public domain image.

glutamate), which excite, inhibit, and modulate visual processing in response to various needs and interests (Guillery & Sherman 2002).

Both the superior colliculus and the lateral geniculate nucleus are information-processing hubs that rapidly organize responses to challenges through their interactions with systems in the cerebellum, brainstem, thalamus, and basal ganglia. Importantly, interactions between these networks and the primary visual cortex (V1) also shape and organize responses to spatially relevant information. The primary visual cortex is present in all mammals, with differences in structure and connectivity reflecting differences in physiological and informational demands (Krubitzer 2007). In each case, V1 preserves the spatial and geometric organization of incoming information. This makes it possible to adjust the salience of edges, orientations, and temporal and spatial frequency by boosting or suppressing activity in cells that respond to specific regions of the visual field; this yields visual pop-out effects, patterns of texture segmentation, and contour enhancement (Desimone & Duncan 1995; Zhaoping 2016).

Crucially, these processes depend upon interactions with numerous subcortical systems. For example, processes centering on the lateral pulvinar – another structure in the thalamus – are employed to enhance the salience of the information in the receptive fields of V1 cells, while suppressing the responsiveness of these cells to surrounding inputs (Purushothaman et al. 2012). At the same time, a brainstem structure known as the locus coeruleus produces norepinephrine, a chemical signal that can enhance neural excitability and modulate visual attention (Waterhouse & Navarra 2019). Finally, ongoing interactions with networks centered on the superior colliculus continually modulate orientations toward salient stimuli, while also guiding various forms of perception and action.

In each of these contexts, multiple networks are employed to regulate and stabilize the flow of visual information. However, a relatively tight connection is preserved between animals and the geometric structure of their environments. Sometimes, spatial maps in the superior colliculus are employed to organize orienting behavior and to calibrate diverse sources of sensory information; sometimes, spatial maps in the lateral geniculate nucleus and V1 are used to organize sensory information for further processing – especially where it is necessary to be sensitive to spatial layouts and the relations between objects (Goodale & Humphrey 1998, 185). Consequently, children who gain sight after extended early-onset blindness respond to the Ponzo and Müller-Lyer illusions in similar ways to congenitally sighted people (Gandhi et al. 2015), and similar patterns of activity are observed in V1 when blind *expert* echolocators *hear* the location of echo sounds and when sighted people *see* the locations of images (Norman & Thaler 2019, 4).

2.4 Attentional, Affective, and Visceral Information

The story we have told thus far focuses on the way that information flows through the superior colliculus, the lateral geniculate nucleus, and V1. But it is important to note that sources of attentional and visceral information are continually integrated into visual processing, beginning at the sensory periphery and proceeding through various cortical and subcortical networks. For example, affective information is initially integrated into sensory processing by peripheral receptors, which boost the *salience* of bitter tastes, decay-related smells, affiliative touch, and tissue damage; further processes then enhance an animal's sensitivity to these kinds of information, prioritizing them without any need for further conceptualization (Kryklywy et al. 2020). Additional affective information is often integrated beyond these initial responses; where this is necessary, subcortical systems that center on the superior colliculus, basal ganglia, amygdala, and locus coeruleus play significant roles in organizing perceptual attention. Collectively, these processes shape everything that happens in cortical systems, and what an animal perceives is continually shaped by expected costs and rewards – and in numerous cases, reward-based information is prioritized across situations, sensory modalities, and stimulus properties.

The precise nature of the processes that modulate attention are complex, but it is clear that subcortical systems play numerous roles in classifying sensory data, integrating evaluative expectations, and producing a dynamic signal of an animal's current state (Schulkin et al. 2003). Hungry people tend to be more attentive to the food they see, and more attentive to their food-related memories (Talmi et al. 2013); people who worry about snakes on a hiking trail tend to see snakes, even where there are none around; and perceptions of race are some-times shaped by feelings of economic precarity (Krosch & Amodio 2014). Likewise, combat veterans returning from Afghanistan often automatically prioritize combat-related stimuli for years after traumatic encounters; moreover, passengers on a flight that narrowly avoided crashing in the Atlantic Ocean tend to be more sensitive to stimuli that are associated with the crash years after the event, even where they are unaware of the relationship between the stimuli and the traumatic memory; finally, many interpersonal relationships will often fall into habitual misunderstandings that reflect the expected salience of ongoing interactions. In each of these cases, and many others besides, learning and habituation will tend to guide perception toward rewarding stimuli, and away from aversive stimuli, in ways that reflect the individuals' histories over numer-ous timescales (Todd & Manaligod 2018).

These patterns of perceptual attention are sustained by dense connections between cortical and subcortical systems. Connections between the superior colliculus and basal ganglia integrate sensory information with evaluative expectations (Krauzlis et al. 2014); in this context, dopamine appears to be the main chemical signal that prioritizes rewarding information and enhances the salience of reward-related information (Anderson 2016). In parallel, nor-epinephrine serves as a chemical signal that can enhance cortical signaling and bias competition between sensory inputs in ways that support implicit atten-tional sets that highlight affectively salient stimuli (Todd & Manaligod 2018, 128). Each of these systems is sensitive to the diverse range of challenges and opportunities that an animal must face. Moreover, these chemical signals are not just used to adjust neural activity in accordance with the current evaluative state of an animal; they also shape future activity in ways that reflect remembered patterns of risks, threats, and rewards. Consequently, what an animal perceives is shaped, in an ongoing way, by diverse forms of attentional salience that are regulated in accordance with expectations about the likely costs and rewards of acting (Huebner 2019; Todd & Manaligod 2018). Put somewhat differently, animals tend to perceive the things that matter to their current and ongoing needs, and visual systems exploit numerous sources of affective and evaluative information to constrain processing over multiple timescales, yielding flexible, context-sensitive responses to numerous different features of the world.

For our purposes, the key thing to notice is that there will always be trade-offs in perception – preserving a connection to geometric stabilities is important to visual processing, but attention must continually be directed toward predators, prey, and other ecologically relevant phenomena – and the resulting patterns of stability and flexibility must be sustained by interactions within complex networks of neural processes, which are dynamically adjusted by chemical signaling systems, in ways that sustain the forms of adaptability that are necessary to survive and flourish in a complex and often dangerous world.

2.5 Cortical Processing

Vision is always a process of identifying things that matter and preparing for interactions that are likely to preserve viability. In frogs and toads, several interacting systems sustain behavioral flexibility in response to ecologically significant stimuli (Ewert et al. 2001); likewise, birds and mammals rely upon flexible interactions between cortical and subcortical processes to sustain ecologically relevant behavior over multiple timescales (Goodale 2011). To get a sense of what this amounts to, we focus on human primates, where visually guided behavior relies upon interactions between cortical and subcortical networks that integrate diverse sources of perceptual, somatosensory, and motor information (Felleman & Van Essen 1991).

Consider someone who is attempting to pick up a coffee cup. It is commonly assumed that this capacity is supported by two partially distinct, but interacting, processing streams (see Figure 7). Processes in the ventral stream are primarily involved in identifying the coffee cup as something to be grasped; processes in the dorsal stream primarily support the real-time guidance of behavior, including the regulation of grasping speed, grip aperture, and reach trajectory; and interactions between these processing streams support our rich sensitivity to every change that occurs as we engage with salient objects (Milner & Goodale 2008; Ungerleider & Pessoa 2018). But to understand what this hypothesis amounts to, it is necessary to examine these processing streams in a bit more detail.

To begin with, processes early within the dorsal stream appear to be sensitive to the geometric structure of the world, as well as stable relations of perspective and predictable patterns of moving bodies (Freud et al. 2016). Some of these

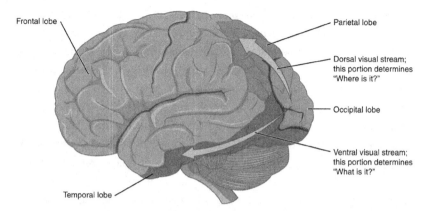

Figure 7 'Visual streams' by OpenStax College, licensed under CC BY 3.0. Wikimedia Commons.

constraints reflect the spatial organization of the lateral geniculate nucleus and the superior colliculus, since directed reaching and grasping are often preserved following damage to V1 (Goodale 2011). But more generally, it appears that the information flowing through this stream is formatted to allow for interactions between the dorsal and ventral stream. In both cases, predictable regularities in spatial organization, along with predictable variations in edges and orientations, have supported the internalization of capacities for tracking changes in position and orientation, which occur as animals move and engage with the world (Shepard 1984). This allows interactions to occur throughout these processing streams, and this means that sensitivities to categorical abstractions can structure and organize ongoing activity across numerous different contexts.

Later in the dorsal stream, activity along a pathway that leads from the visual cortex to the prefrontal cortex appears to use visual information to stabilize spatial working memory over time, activity along a pathway that leads from the visual cortex to the premotor cortex appears to sustain rapid visually guided action, and activity along a pathway that leads from the visual cortex to the medial temporal lobe appears to support navigation (Kravitz et al. 2011). In each of these cases, egocentric spatial maps are employed, which allow for the integration of various forms of categorical information. But processes in the third pathway transform egocentric information into depictions of 'distant space' that are less sensitive to the demands of immediate action guidance and to changes in somatosensory information. This transformation is important to ongoing behavioral guidance and, since this third pathway terminates in the medial temporal lobe, it can integrate information about the dynamic relationships between head direction, orientation, and location into more complex cognitive maps (O'Keefe & Nadel 1978). Finally, since these processes operate in parallel, egocentric information about what specific things look like *from here* can be integrated with allocentric information about how things look relative to distant space, making it possible to sustain perspectival orientations relative to landmarks while preserving a heading across changes in the flow of visual information

Things are more complex in the ventral stream. Many of us can accurately identify and engage with ecologically novel objects such as cars, cookies, and coffee cups. It is implausible to posit innate capacities for tracking and responding to such stimuli, but many of us perceive the invariant features of such objects across changes in their position, orientation, and illumination that make each encounter with these ecologically novel objects almost unique (DiCarlo et al. 2012). Many researchers assume that the only way to account for these abilities is by appealing to constructive computations within the ventral stream, which can transform noisy retinal images into categorical representations of objects and events. It is worth noting that this view is a modern descendent of the constructive theory of vision that we explored in Section 2.1.

According to this framework, perceptual learning is assumed to exploit networks of computational operations that adjust firing rates and neural dynamics to produce a stable model of the world. Since adjacent stimuli typically activate adjacent neurons, the spatial organization of information can be fed forward through multiple processing stages. Moreover, it seems that these spatial maps are overlaid with feature maps that encode color, orientation, movement, and more. These maps can be used to enhance the salience of specific features in specific locations in the visual field (Itti & Koch 2000). Finally, back-propagations through this processing stream can be used to minimize the impact of visual clutter and ambiguous stimuli by directing attention to salient stimuli (Serre et al. 2007).

None of this entails, or even requires, that constructive processes are employed in the ventral stream, but these structural constraints could sustain gradual transformations of impoverished retinal signals, yielding increasingly abstract representations of the things that matter to an animal – including cars, cookies, and coffee (DiCarlo et al. 2012). From this perspective, the processes involved in perceiving these phenomena might seem to be analogous to deep neural networks of the sort that are employed in the context of machine learning. This is intriguing, as a pattern of organization that looks a lot like the ventral stream has been observed after training a deep neural network on video from head-mounted cameras worn by crawling infants (Zhuang et al. 2021), but we should proceed cautiously. We have little idea how these patterns of activity sustain *active and engaged* perception. These videos capture some of the core dynamics of visual scenes, and it seems likely that a deep neural network could sustain passive viewing. But crawling infants are not passive observers; they are active and engaged perceivers who integrate proprioceptive, visual, auditory, olfactory, hedonic, and motivational information, and they do so while navigating actual and potential obstacles. So before we claim that there are interesting similarities between deep neural networks and biological systems, we should be sure that the activity of the ventral stream is: (1) resilient across changes in the interactions between the subcortical and cortical processes that dynamically organize active and engaged perception; and (2) resilient across changes in the interactions between the dorsal and ventral streams, which are necessary for monitoring changes in spatial information, directing attention toward salient features of the world, and keeping track of the locations of various obstacles and challenges (Milner 2017).

Against this backdrop, we might ask: What does it mean to claim that the neural structures in the ventral stream instantiate something like a deep neural network? First, this claim can be interpreted as proposing that the ventral stream *constructs* representations of categories – this is a relatively standard approach. But, second, we can interpret this as a claim about a system that *adapts* to observable structures in the available inputs (Davies-Barton et al. 2022). Adopting this second approach makes it possible to understand these processes as reflecting the internalization of perceptual constraints that sustain capacities to track available information through active engagements with the local environment. Drawing upon the analogy to a complex network of analog and digital pedals that we developed in Section 2.2, we might say that the settings on different effects are adjusted over the course of development to bring the output of the visual system into alignment with the sources of information that are most relevant to viability. For example, category-specific sensitivities to faces, bodies, tools, objects, numerals, visual word forms, and landmarks might be organized by three kinds of interacting constraints: (1) features of stimuli can constrain the forms of information processing that are carried out; (2) patterns of neural connectivity can constrain the flow of information through the brain; and (3) operations that occur earlier in the visual system can constrain what is done as information flows through subsequent processes (Op de Beeck et al. 2019, 784).

Consider the fact that many people rapidly perceive faces. This is possible because faces have a distinctive feature-based geometry that constrains information processing. Furthermore, processes that occur earlier in the ventral stream are more sensitive to information about lines, orientations, and curvature, while processes later in the ventral stream appear to be sensitive to configurations of features. Since people typically have numerous encounters with faces over the course of development, they could internalize constraints that allow them to become attuned to the geometric configuration of faces

(Op de Beeck et al. 2019, 789). Put much too simply, this would occur because adjustments are made over the course of development, yielding a cascade of processes that first track lines, orientations, and curvature, and later track the geometric configuration of faces – yielding processes centered on the fusiform gyrus that are attuned to the tracking of faces (Kanwisher & Yovel 2006).

Color vision is another context where ecological challenges lead to the internalization of processing constraints. As Evan Thompson (1995) argues, there is no single property that color vision always responds to. In fish, color vision highlights differences between foreground objects and background light, and it sometimes sustains capacities to detect bioluminescent bacteria. Many birds rely upon color vision to track aesthetic qualities and attend to silhouettes against brightly and dimly lit skies (for defenses of similar claims see Marler 2000 and Prum 2017). Honeybees use color vision to guide foraging decisions by tracking patterns of ultraviolet light that are invisible to humans. Finally, different patterns of color responsiveness within and between primate species sustain differences in capacities for object detection and scene segmentation. In each context, interactions between specialized eyes, photoreceptors, and opsin genes have been calibrated over evolutionary timescales to track the opportunities and challenges that matter to survival and flourishing; color vision is an integral part of this process, as it distinguishes many of the features of the world that satisfy a perceiver's ecological needs (Thompson 1995). With this claim in mind, consider some intriguing data regarding *C. elegans*, a roundworm that lacks specialized eyes, photoreceptors, and opsin genes. These roundworms respond to variations in the relative intensity of blue and amber light, which are commonly associated with toxins in their environments (Ghosh et al. 2021). It is unlikely that they perceive colors in exactly the way that humans tend to, but they are able to track and respond to sources of color information that are relevant to surviving in their ecological niche.

2.6 Perceptual Integration

Summarizing our claims thus far, a biological perspective on perception should not be restricted to forms of categorization. Nor should it assume that perception presents disaggregated patterns of color, faces, and objects in typical context. Instead, it should understand perception as bringing an animal into contact with biologically relevant features of a world. But how are the diverse sources of perceptually relevant information from other sensory systems integrated into a unified form of awareness of a world, rather than an awareness of sensory particulars?

In addressing this question, it might help to consider the fact that Blind people and sighted people who learn Braille under conditions of prolonged visual deprivation use similar networks in V1 to read Braille texts (Merabet et al. 2008). Likewise, similar regions of the cortex are used when congenitally Blind people read Braille and when sighted people read visually presented text (Reich et al. 2011). Finally, similar cortical processes are used when Blind people localize category-specific sounds or tactile stimuli and when sighted people localize category-specific images (Op de Beeck 2019, 790). Such data suggest that there are spatial constraints that shape perceptual processing across various sensory modalities. However, just as importantly, the connections between V1 and other cortical regions are often substantially different in Blind and sighted people (Striem-Amit et al. 2015). Indeed, much of the available data suggest that different processing strategies can be used to track and respond to similar kinds of spatial information, which is one of the main things that vision does in typical contexts.

When visual information is lacking or diminished, other sensory systems are often recruited to sustain successful navigation. As Nicholas Giudice (2018) – a Blind vision scientist – reminds us, people who are Blind or visually impaired are often able to: (1) detect and avoid obstacles; (2) determine intersection geometry as well as the state of traffic signals, and orient in ways that allow them to safely cross busy streets; and (3) maintain an ongoing awareness of salient landmarks. In these contexts, and many others besides, other sensory systems are used to compensate for visual deficits. For example, when a Blind or visually impaired person walks from a hotel to a nearby bakery, they might rely upon:

> echo location from their cane or foot steps to determine the position and distance of the trashcan as they pass, the sound of people eating to identify the location and direction of the tables at the café, the feel of texture changes from a tactile warning strip to indicate the presence of the intersection and the correct orientation to adopt for a safe street crossing, the auditory flow of passing cars to assess the state of the traffic signal, the smell of the bakery as a cue that they are nearing the destination (Giudice 2018, 275).

Diverse sources of perceptual information are processed and integrated to guide active and engaged perception. However, different processes can be employed to navigate different challenges and opportunities. This yields a key insight about perceptual integration in the context of biological cognition: mobile animals must keep track of the spatial layout of their sensory environment, but where this information comes from is often less important than whether diverse sources of information can be flexibly integrated to yield a coherent awareness of the challenges that must be faced and the available opportunities.

In the context of active and engaged perception, it is often necessary to adjust perceptual processing to manage the challenges and opportunities that arise. Nonetheless, a tight connection is preserved between the sources of information that are available to an agent and the networks of evolved and learned constraints that shape information processing. Put somewhat differently, since the photons hitting the retina do not constitute an impoverished source of information, constructive operations need not be employed to produce representations of a world filled with colors, textures, and opportunities. Like Gibson, we thus hold that perception is an active process that brings animals into contact with challenges and opportunities, but unlike Gibson, we also hold that numerous processes are used to manipulate perceptual inputs and to produce behavioral and cognitive effects. On the one hand, physiological and ecological constraints on perception stabilize the kinds of things that particular animals perceive. On the other hand, patterns of neural activity are continually adjusted against one another in ways that are shaped by numerous chemical messengers, so different source of information can be upregulated or downregulated to achieve a predictively coherent experience of challenges that must be faced and available opportunities. This yields some degree of flexibility among a broader sea of perceptual stabilities.

We can get a sense of what this means by considering the fact that losing vision later in life often increases the likelihood of psychosis, while congenital blindness might buffer against psychosis (Pollak & Corlett 2020). Managing the challenges that are associated with blindness at different points in life is likely to impose different kinds of burdens on cognition. Many Blind people learn early in life that the world is noisy and complex, and that effort is needed to integrate diverse sources of information, so they are less likely to boost the salience of noisy information. By contrast, a sighted person who learns to perceive the locations of persisting objects within an allocentric space will also learn to reflexively boost the salience of partially glimpsed or distorted images as a way to compensate for visual distortions. Consequently, losing vision later in life will often lead to more patterns of perceptual boosting in contexts where something has been partially glimpsed and in contexts where visual information is noisy or indeterminate. As a result, a person who loses vision later in light might experience more perceptual hallucinations. In this context, and many others besides, diverse neural systems are employed to manage flows of perceptual information. They boost, suppress, filter, and integrate diverse sources of perceptual information, and they do so in ways that are sensitive to the demands of survival and flourishing.

Some of these processes employ analog computations that manage the flow of information. These are not constructive processes, but they do boost, suppress, and filter particular sources of information that are relevant to ongoing behavior. Other processes attempt to stabilize particular sources of information in ways that track higher-level regularities and produce visual experiences in contexts like dreaming and hallucinating. But each of these processes is continually shaped by the activity of processes centered on the amygdala, basal ganglia, hypothalamus, thalamus, and locus coeruleus (Ungerleider & Pessoa 2018), and diverse chemical messengers are employed to manage the flow of information by organizing, prioritizing, and identifying things that matter. Finally, attention appears to increase in the context of more abstract sources of information, leading behavioral relevance to be prioritized over accuracy (Carrasco 2011, 1485). In every case, perceiving is thus a matter of perceiving what matters.

Perceiving the world is only one part of biological cognition. Animals are biologically prepared to track and respond to some kinds of challenges and opportunities, but they must also learn about many other aspects of the world. In the next section, we examine some of the ways that animals learn about the things that matter to survival and flourishing. Building on the framework that we articulated in Section 1, we explore the tight connection between learning about the world and regulating the internal milieu.

3 Learning What Matters

William James (1890) famously asks readers to consider the behavior of a frog who takes the shortest path to the surface when they are placed in a jar of water. When an obstacle is placed in this frog's path, they will explore the area around this obstacle, swim downward, and try other paths until they find a way to the surface. The frog needs oxygen, and this need constrains their behavior. But just as importantly, James argues that the frog is able to vary their means of satisfying this need, and he treats the frog's sensitivity to unexpected challenges as evidence of intelligence. For James, adjusting behavior to achieve a fixed end is the best evidence of cognitive activity. Unfortunately, there are numerous difficulties that arise in adopting this approach to cognition. Most significantly, there seem to be cases where behavior that initially looks intelligent turns out to be rigid and tropistic on further analysis.

Consider the sphex wasp, who stings a cricket and carries it to their nest as they prepare to lay their eggs. When this wasp arrives at their nest, they will examine it for predators, drag the paralyzed cricket inside, then lay their eggs next to the paralyzed cricket, before sealing the door. When the grubs hatch, they eat the paralyzed cricket and open the door, and the process repeats over the course of many lifecycles. This looks like intelligent behavior. But according to a well-known story, if an experimenter moves the paralyzed cricket while the wasp is inspecting their nest, the wasp will repeat their examination of the nest, and this can be done repeatedly, yielding an endless behavioral loop within a single lifetime. This story has often been used to show that apparently intelligent behavior can be supported by reflexive and automatic processes that operate in the absence of cognition or consciousness. Indeed, Daniel Dennett (1995) uses it to support his claim that many kinds of human behavior are sphexish.

This is an intriguing suggestion. But the data in support of this sphex story have always been equivocal, and there has never been any consensus on which aspects of behavior are fixed and which are variable (Keijzer 2013). In some respects, this shouldn't be surprising. Even in cases where behavioral constraints are resilient to change, animals must learn how to respond to locally significant challenges and opportunities. In the early twentieth century, Charles Henry Turner showed that insects can push beyond habit and instinct to navigate unexpected challenges (see Abramson 2009 for a review). This makes sense. Where ecological challenges and opportunities are stable, they should shape an animal's instincts, but they should also shape patterns of learning and curiosity (Tinbergen 1951). Moreover, the complexity of the interactions between ecological, neural, and chemical processes always leave room for flexible learning capacities, which can operate over evolutionary as well as developmental timescales (Tinbergen 1953).

Behavioral flexibility can be important in the context of biological cognition – as James suggests. But the prevalence of relatively fixed behavioral constraints should not be counted as evidence that a process is not cognitively significant. What matters is that a capacity is good enough to facilitate the navigation of the challenges and opportunities that structure an animal's world. Sometimes it is important to internalize constraints; sometimes it is important to remain flexible, so, in general, the study of biological cognition is likely to reveal complex networks of processes, some of which are resilient to variations across contexts, some of which are fragile and dependent on ecological cues. This makes it unlikely that there will be a bright dividing line between which processes are cognitive and which are not; instead, we should expect to find a continuum of processes that allow animals to navigate their ecological niche. But what does this mean?

In all biological contexts, the ability to navigate challenges and opportunities is shaped by evolutionary and developmental constraints. For example, since animals must figure out when and what to eat, they will often be *prepared* to learn which associations in their ecological niche are informative with regard to food (Rozin & Kalat 1971; Seligman 1971). Rats thus display capacities for one-trial learning when a novel flavor is paired with a toxin, but it takes longer for them to learn how electrical shocks are associated with the same toxins (Garcia & Koelling 1966). Likewise, rats find it easier to learn about differences in tastes and smells than to learn about visual cues; by contrast, bobwhite quails find visual cues more salient (Wilcoxon et al. 1971). Over evolutionary time-scales, rats have needed to pair tastes and smells with toxins to survive and flourish; by contrast, quails have needed to decide whether something is worth eating from a distance, because predation risk tends to increase when they pick up food. Finally, encounters with electricity are evolutionarily recent and rare. So, while rats can learn which cues are associated with electrical shocks, they do so by forming assumptions, experiencing feedback, and correcting mistakes where possible.

Such phenomena, and others like them, suggest that resilient behavioral capacities will depend on evolved constraints on learnability (Cummins & Cummins 1999), but there are significant ongoing disputes about the nature of these constraints (Heyes et al. 2020). Many animals are also information seekers who exploit the logical and perceptual relations among stimuli to form a more sophisticated understanding of the world (Rescorla 1988, 154). In this section, our aim is to suggest that biological cognition is organized by three kinds of constraints on learning: features of stimuli constrain which forms of information processing must be carried out (Section 3.1); constraints on physiological regulation determine which demands must be satisfied at a specific point in time (Section 3.2); and the kinds of cognitive and regulatory processes that occur in a specific context constrain how information flows through an embodied animal (Sections 3.3–4.2).

3.1 Sodium Regulation

Sodium regulation has long served as a model of biological learning. This makes sense: Sodium hunger is an essential aspect of biological cognition, since salty tastes reliably indicate the presence of other essential minerals (Schulkin 1991). When rats are deprived of sodium, they ingest salt within moments of first encountering it (Wolf 1969). But animals are not only prepared to recognize salt, they are also prepared to learn which tastes and actions are associated with sodium and to track the features that facilitate acquiring sodium in different contexts (compare Rescorla 1980). Sodium is a biologically signifi-cant resource, and decades of research has revealed that the craving for salt impacts viability across numerous contexts.

Ungulates will travel long distances to reach salt licks, even if doing so increases the likelihood of predation (Denton 1982). When they discover plausible sources of sodium, they will return to them frequently. Moreover, when familiar sodium sources are depleted, increased levels of a chemical signal (aldosterone) lead many animals – including rabbits, kangaroos, and wombats – to seek alternative sources of salt (Blair-West et al. 1968). Such behavior requires remembering viable paths and trajectories, locating familiar resources, and exploring alternatives when familiar sodium sources have been depleted. But no less importantly, changes in the need for sodium tend to modulate affective appraisals, rendering sodium and related tastes more palatable (Berridge & Schulkin 1989; Berridge et al. 1984), and the initiation of behavior to restore viable levels of water and sodium depends on chemical signaling systems that evoke context-sensitive shifts in sodium excretion and sodium conservation (Daniels & Schulkin 2018).

Focusing on these latter processes reveals complex cascades of physiological activity that shapes cognition and behavior over multiple timescales. Receptors that signal decreased blood volume and changes in the body's electrolyte–water balance regulate salt and water levels fairly directly (Denton 1982; Fitzsimons 1979). At the same time, variations in sodium availability adjust the secretion of renin from the kidneys, and increased blood pressure – which is triggered by the interaction between chemical messengers (renin/angiotensin) – motivates the search for water and sodium (Epstein 1982). The search for water is immediate, and it is induced directly by angiotensin. Aldosterone then facilitates further expression of angiotensin in the brain, which motivates the search for water and salt. But, since the search for salt typically unfolds along longer timescales, additional chemical signals (steroids and aldosterone) must be deployed to organize the retention of sodium and the redistribution of mineral resources throughout the body. The interaction between all of these processes produces sodium cravings and organizes their salience, while also motivating the search for salt and other essential minerals (Geerling & Loewy 2008).

This story might already seem to be complex, but there are numerous further complexities to explore. Chemical signals play multiple roles in behavioral and physiological regulation, so it is difficult to develop a unified model of neural and chemical signaling. Consider the fact that the same chemical signal that promotes the search for salt also regulates the ingestion of salt. Something similar occurs in the context of phosphate depletion, which can induce tremors and the breakdown of motor capabilities. Such challenges can be avoided by attempting to reestablish homeostasis when phosphate levels change, but they can also be avoided through anticipatory regulation. Both strategies are used, and they are both mediated by the same molecules, which affect the kidneys and the brain in different ways: In the kidneys, they promote phosphate conservation; in the brain, they promote behavior that leads to phosphate ingestion

(Mulroney et al. 2004). In each of these cases, we cannot be content with a simple or unified appeal to a chemical signal – instead, we need to ask what a chemical does in a particular context and how it shapes activity in a particular regulatory network.

3.2 Physiological Regulation and Cognition

Of course, sodium and phosphate are not the only variables that need to be managed. Indeed, the processes that are involved in thermoregulation, thirst regulation, hunger regulation, and the regulation of appetites for diverse minerals (salt, calcium, phosphate) must often be managed in parallel as animals prepare to address various challenges and opportunities. Fortunately, many of these processes are anchored to relatively stable cycles of activity, which are regulated by hypothalamic and extrahypothalamic regions of the brain. These cycles of activity initiate metabolic processes that break down stores of energy when it is time to forage, and they shift to energy storage when it is time to rest, repair, and grow (Schulkin & Sterling 2019, 741). These forms of anticipatory regulation are typically supported by adjustments to chemical signals (hormones), which typically occur on a predictable timetable. But these processes can also be calibrated against predictable ecological regularities.

For example, when eating occurs on a fixed schedule, the secretion of chemical signals such as cortisol and leptin can become anchored to stable rhythms, which will regulate the desire for food and the willingness to eat. But where access to food and nutrients is more variable, these same processes will be calibrated against perceptual regularities and activities. Simplifying somewhat, many animals learn to track the times of day when they typically have access to food, along with the sounds, visual cues, and tastes that reliably co-occur with food, and these forms of learning rely upon the calibration of numerous physiological processes that prepare animals to digest their preferred foods.

One part of this process concerns the secretion of insulin in anticipation of eating. This chemical signal prepares cells to absorb glucose, it prepares the gastrointestinal tract to break down fats and proteins, and it motivates food-driven thought and behavior (Dallman et al. 1993; Woods et al. 1977). Intriguingly, preferences appear to shape this response directly. As rats learn to avoid sweet tastes that make them sick, the anticipatory secretion of insulin is adjusted, triggering changes in both consumption and species-specific displays of pleasure and displeasure (Berridge et al. 1981). Likewise, perceiving palatable foods triggers cascades of digestive and metabolic responses in hungry animals, preparing their bodies to digest, absorb, and metabolize nutrients

(Pavlov 1902); and here, too, palatability seems to directly affect regulatory processing (Powley 1977). This is possible because regulatory processes are tightly coupled to the taste of food, to the motivation to feed where things taste pleasant, and to tendencies to inhibit eating where potentially toxic or tainted foods are ingested (Power & Schulkin 2008).

Taste matters because it shapes and is shaped by the regulation of physiological demands. But importantly, regulation should not be understood simply as a process of correcting mistakes, as it tends to be within more Bayesian frameworks. Nor should it be seen as passive responses to changes in the world. Physiological activities are actively shaped by effort, action, and perception; they require a sensitivity to trade-offs between different regulatory needs, as well as ongoing attempts to stabilize physiological variables, and, collectively, these factors allow species-typical tendencies to be calibrated in ways that are sensitive to diverse activities and salient physiological demands. This was shown in the work of Curt Richter (1943, 1956). Richter showed that rats drink excessive amounts of water to stabilize their internal milieu when they are unable to regulate levels of an antidiuretic hormone (*vasopressin*) because their pituitary glands have been damaged. He also showed that rats will find and ingest sodium to preserve viability when they secrete excessive quantities of sodium. Across numerous biological contexts, including the regulation of phosphorus, calcium, carbohydrates, and fats, Richter found similar results, and this suggests that physiological regulation is active, context sensitive, and governed by dense feedback loops between the brain and the rest of the body.

With these claims in mind, it will help to return briefly to questions about learning what and when to eat. Wild rat pups are reluctant to eat foods that have not been introduced to them, so they must learn what to eat from older members of their colony (see Galef & Laland 2005 for a review). This form of learning is scaffolded by adult rats, who convey information about their preferences by marking the foods they eat with olfactory cues. But, curiously, even preferences for noxious foods like garlic can be passed from a pregnant rat to her pups, and this can occur even where pups are cross-fostered by rats who have never eaten garlic (Hepper 1988, cited in Galef & Laland 2005). This is surprising from a perspective that focuses only on learning, but if constraints can be internalized over the course of development, then perhaps physiological processes that are operative prior to birth can shape initial food preferences, at least in rats. Once such preferences are in place, it would then be possible for teaching and learning to enhance preferences for foods that conspecifics eat. Perhaps surprisingly, teaching will rarely generate new preferences (Laland 1993), but the social enhancement of preferences can and does help animals to overcome learned as well as species-typical aversions to specific foods that become socially preferable.

Something similar seems to occur in the human context. Some human preferences are anchored to specific nutrients and energy-rich foods. Such preferences might be shaped by constraints that have been internalized over evolutionary timescales, but many human preferences are also shaped by social learning, and interactions between biological and social needs (Rozin & Schulkin 1990). Over the course of development, dynamic feedback between biological needs, endogenous preferences, and social cues organizes the pursuit of specific foods, as well as relative preferences for specific foods, and these preferences are continually shaped by sensory and affective information, by anticipations regarding the potential consequences of eating specific foods, and by more cognitive assumptions about what it means to ingest particular things (Rozin 1990). A detailed exploration of the processes that calibrate food preferences would shed a great deal of light on human learning and human social cognition, and we return to this issue briefly below (Section 4.2). But, for now, we must rest content with the claim that the stability of food preferences will always reflect the combined influence of individual differences, species-typical capacities for social learning, and social dynamics, all of which shape the pursuit of viability in specific environments (Galef & Laland 2005).

It is difficult to articulate precise and general models of biological and social regulation (Brown et al. 2020), and you might be wondering whether these problems only arise in the context of digestion and regulation. Digestion and regulation are rarely considered *cognitive* activities. Of course, every cognitively significant aspect of eating and regulating unfolds against the backdrop of these processes, which must be calibrated to be responsive to ecological challenges and opportunities. Moreover, these processes must often be managed in parallel, in ways that are sensitive to the challenges and opportunities that arise in unpredictable environments. But it is worth considering the possibility that a more unified story about the kinds of learning that are commonly studied in psychology and the cognitive sciences can be layered atop these regulatory demands.

3.3 A Unified Story about Learning?

Animals seem to learn how their actions are associated with affectively relevant outcomes, and they seem to do so by forming expectations and revising these expectations when unexpected things happen (Rescorla 1988). These patterns of learning are stable across different contexts, and numerous models of behavior have been constructed to explain how animals improve their *estimates* of where, when, and how much *reward* an action will yield. Many of these models suggest that *expectations* are adjusted in light of *reward-prediction errors* (Dayan & Niv 2008). For example, according to one well-known model: Prediction-error signals are evoked by differences between predicted and actual rewards; larger error signals produce larger changes in association strength; and association strength is increased when outcomes are better than expected, and decreased when outcomes are worse than expected (Rescorla & Wagner 1972). This process requires extensive feedback to support learning in real-world environments, and it often yields suboptimal outputs where good actions have typically led to undesirable outcomes and where bad actions have led to desirable outcomes. However, in the 1990s evidence began to accumulate suggesting that dopaminergic neurons in the primate midbrain were responsive to differences between expected and actual rewards in just this way (Montague et al. 1996; Schultz 2010).

This was an exciting development. It suggested a way to integrate physiological data with careful observations of learning. Moreover, further data soon emerged suggesting that nearby processes were adjusting expectations in contexts where rewards were less certain and where actions were riskier, and computational strategies were proposed to supplement these systems with model-based computations (using graphical models or decision trees) that represented salient features of an environment, transitions between various states, and the predicted consequences of different actions. Finally, it was proposed that interactions between these systems supported observable capacities for making ecologically and socially relevant decisions (Montague 2007; Railton 2017), and it seemed clear that the cognitive sciences were on the verge of explaining how animals attune to their ecological and social worlds (Huebner 2016). But note, this story says little about how features of stimuli constrain information processing, how diverse demands must be satisfied at different points in time, or which kinds of regulatory processing might constrain the flow of information through an embodied animal.

Consequently, it should come as no surprise that there are several obstacles that stand in the way of establishing a tight connection between specific algorithms and patterns of neural activity (Dayan & Niv 2008; Hayden & Niv 2021). For example, patterns of neural activity that look like prediction errors are just as common for novel events as they are for rewarding events (Liljeholm and O'Doherty 2012); moreover, dopamine depletion affects task performance and incentive salience without affecting learning (Berridge 2012), and even where dopamine plays a role in learning about the temporal relations between actions and outcomes (in mice), it isn't as tightly coupled to *reward* as people commonly assume (Sharpe et al. 2020). Finally, when sub-second dopamine fluctuations were monitored in Parkinson's patients undergoing brain surgery, they were not directly correlated with reward-prediction errors; the best model of these fluctuations reflected the integration of reward-prediction errors with *counterfactual* predictions about how much better or worse an outcome *could* have been (Kishida et al. 2016). It is risky to generalize from these data, since Parkinson's disease results from impaired dopamine function, and alternative computational models might capture these data but yield a very different interpretation (Platt & Pearson 2016). Nonetheless, they point to a significant complication in mapping patterns of learning directly onto neural and chemical data.

To be clear, the claim that processes centered on midbrain structures such as the basal ganglia organize some patterns of thought and behavior continues to seem plausible (compare Bechtel & Huang 2022). Moreover, interactions between subcortical and cortical systems appear to shape learning and salience, as well as tendencies to approach and avoid particular situations. But chemical signaling systems operate in ways that diverge quite radically from the identifiable patterns of cellular activity that are typically highlighted by computational approaches to cognition. For example, variations in the amount of available dopamine shape everything from motor behavior to impulsivity and motivation, and variations in this chemical signal are involved in numerous psychological difficulties ranging from addiction to ADHD and schizophrenia. Across these contexts, this chemical signal plays numerous different roles, and at the level of cellular activity it can function either as a neurotransmitter or as a diffuse chemical signal that will either boost or suppress synaptic signaling depending on where and when it happens to bind to a receptor. This is typically the case with chemical signals. Even where they are released and used locally, they often affect different cells in different ways, and they can evoke different cascades of neural activity as a function of the amount of the chemical signal that is present, as well as the point on a receptive cell where the chemical happens to bind (Shine et al. 2022).

Just as importantly, learning depends upon ongoing interactions between numerous systems that are distributed throughout the brain and body. This is true in contexts like eating and the regulation of sodium and potassium, but it is also true in the context of becoming more attuned to social regularities and social opportunities. Attempts to posit distinct computational signals must therefore cross a high bar. They must be stable across diverse behaviors and contexts while remaining sensitive to changes in physiological demands. This makes it unlikely that a specific neural process will code for reward, and this will be true even if animals must be sensitive to the patterns of reward in their local environments. We thus propose that an adequate account of learning will require explaining how fluid interactions between numerous systems are adjusted by diverse chemical signals, it will require explaining how these adjustments are made to manage specific challenges and opportunities, and finally it will need to be sensitive to the complex forms of affect that are integrated into cognition to guide ecologically and socially salient behavior. This doesn't make for a simple or unified story, but it is the only story that can be told about biological cognition.

3.4 Learning about Threats and Dangers

Consider the ability to learn about threats and dangers. Avoiding dangerous snakes is often adaptive, but when an aversion to snakes dominates someone's thinking, and leads them to perceive innocuous objects as dangerous, this same response can be maladaptive. Likewise, being on high alert in some social contexts is adaptive, but prolonged experiences of social anxiety make it difficult to cope with mundane challenges. Finally, where disgust pulls an animal away from toxic substances, it can play a critical role in the preservation of viability, but where social disgust evokes hostility toward others, similar feelings can support pervasive patterns of oppression, exclusion, and marginalization.

According to one recent hypothesis, emotions such as fear are supported by complex patterns of neural activity, which are only unified by conceptual representations, or other kinds of high-level expectations. From this perspective, a person might perceive a rope as a snake because they expect snakes to be around, or they might misperceive a cell phone as a gun because they expect people who are racialized as black to be dangerous. In such contexts, and many others as well, expectations (including conceptual expectations) might shape patterns of physiological regulation, yielding emotional experiences (Barrett 2017); if so, then focusing on the role of such expectations would offer a plausible explanation of the similarities and differences between typical and pathological affective profiles.

According to another hypothesis, it seems likely that there is a much tighter connection between the neural and chemical processes that produce emotions and the specific kinds of challenges and responses they support. If this is the case, we should find that affective processes are tightly coupled to specific kinds of bodily and neural systems, which are flexibly integrated to facilitate successful engagements with the challenges and opportunities that an animal must face. Just as importantly, we should expect such processes to explain the production of anxious and apprehensive thoughts, increased sensitivities to threats and dangers, and motivations to fight, flee, or freeze. This approach would make room for conceptual expectations to play a role in boosting or suppressing particular kinds of affective responses, but it would do so in a way that fits comfortably with the approach to perception that we articulated in the previous section.

A defense of this approach might begin by noting that the amygdala plays a crucial role in producing fear responses and navigating social and ecological threats across species (Ledoux & Brown 2017). Like most neural systems, the boundaries of the amygdala are difficult to specify (Figure 8), but processes that recruit structures in this area are involved in integrating diverse sources of visceral, cognitive, and affective information (Davis & Whalen 2001; Schulkin et al. 2003; Swanson & Petrovich 1998). This structure can be recruited in evaluative learning; it is involved in the regulation of appetitive motivation, vigilance, attentional salience, and changes in motor behavior; and it is involved in the production of the forms of attention and cognitive processing that are associated with experiences of fear and aversion. The key thing to notice here is that these amygdalar systems are a processing hub, which is important for regulating attention and learning, assessing and evaluating information, and motivating action (Pessoa 2010).

In the context of typical and pathological fear, processes that involve the amygdala, midbrain, and brainstem organize the behavioral, autonomic, and endocrine responses that are necessary to manage various threats and dangers (Rosen & Schulkin 1998). This includes various changes in heart rate, blood pressure, and respiration; it also includes shifts in perceptual attention, and

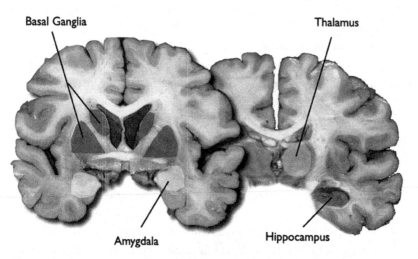

Figure 8 The amygdala, Basal ganglia, hippocampus, and thalamus are key subcortical structures that are involved in learning what matters.
Image courtesy of John Kubie.

physiological changes that support preparation to fight or flee; finally, it includes changes in cognitive processing that are directed toward managing currently salient challenges. All of these effects are regulated by chemical messengers that are expressed in the central amygdala: corticotrophin-releasing hormone and glucocorticoids (Schulkin 2006).

Experiences of losing control and experiences of distress tend to evoke the secretion of glucocorticoids. Likewise, circulating levels of corticotrophin-releasing hormone are routinely linked to experiences of fear and uncertainty, and infusions of corticotrophin-releasing hormone evoke the complex cascade of fear responses we have just discussed. Each of these chemical messengers is produced in anticipation of threats, stressors, and challenges to viability. Such responses are adaptive where they are sensitive to actual challenges, but prolonged and exaggerated activity in these processes can also support the chronic anticipation of negative events, along with the persisting forms of physiological arousal that are common in the context of affective disorders (Schulkin et al. 1994). Furthermore, corticotrophin-releasing hormone plays different roles in different neural contexts (Baumgartner et al. 2021). For example, processes centered on the central amygdala and basal ganglia use corticotrophin-releasing hormone to increase incentive salience and motivate the pursuit of rewards; by contrast, systems in the bed nucleus of the stria terminalis use this chemical signal to produce aversive responses and avoidance behaviors, and to suppress the motivation to pursue rewards. This point is key – chemical signals play different roles in different contexts, and understanding what roles they play requires attending to physiological organization in a way that few computational perspectives have done.

This is not to deny that there are clearly specifiable roles that chemical signals play. One way to see this is to consider what happens when regulatory systems stabilize in problematic ways. For example, consider the way that early neglect and abuse increase the risk of behavioral and emotional problems for humans. Children who experience frequent bouts of acute stress as the result of growing up under adverse conditions are more likely to develop fearful and vigilant emotional profiles, and they are more likely to adopt impulsive and habitual behavioral strategies (Gunnar 2017). These long-term changes in thought and behavior are the effect of an extended developmental period – perhaps lasting through puberty – where the regulation of social stress is calibrated in response to the likelihood of experiencing stressful and traumatic events (Gunnar & Fisher 2006). In the short run, failing to resolve stress responses is adaptive, as stress alerts children to the dangers they are likely to encounter; but in the long run, where these tendencies stabilize as maladaptive responses, they produce troubling forms of experience as well as more reactive patterns of social engagement.

Social stressors including social threats, feelings of abandonment, and the sense that things are out of control all tend to evoke increased activity along the hypothalamic–pituitary–adrenal axis, recruiting processes that are centered on the amygdala and the bed nucleus of the stria terminalis (Figure 9). The activity in these systems constitutes a multistage process, where neurons in the hypothalamus release two chemical signals to initiate cognitive and behavioral responses (corticotrophin-releasing hormone; arginine vasopressin). This triggers the release of a third chemical signal in the pituitary gland (adrenocorticotropic hormone), shifting blood pressure, managing blood glucose levels, and initiating the production of a final chemical signal (glucocorticoids) in the adrenal cortex, thus triggering bodily processes including the fight-or-flight response. Collectively, these processes support the physiological, behavioral, and cognitive changes that prepare an animal to face stressors, threats, and challenges to viability (Gunnar & Quevedo 2007; McEwen 1998, 2004). Over shorter timescales, this cascade of chemical signals sustains rapid shifts in attention and motivates behavioral responses; over longer timescales, the final chemical messengers (glucocorticoids) inhibit the production of corticotrophin-releasing hormone, leading to a reversal of this chemical cascade and a reestablishment of a viable state after a challenge has been managed (McEwen & Seeman 1999; Sapolsky et al. 2000).

Strikingly, people with chronic experiences of PTSD will often have circulating levels of the steroid hormone cortisol that are lower than expected, as well as central levels of corticotrophin-releasing hormone that are higher than expected (Yehuda & Ledoux 2007). These lower levels of circulating cortisol appear to be an effect of individual physiological differences that emerge early in development, but they have a massive effect on experience and cognition. Specifically, lower circulating cortisol levels at the time of a traumatic event tend to support higher levels of norepinephrine, which shape the encoding and consolidating of trauma-related memories; thus, traumatic memories tend to be encoded along with heightened feelings of distress. From here, every act of re-retrieval in a high-stress context will perpetuate anxiety, distress, and more reactive responses to apparent threats, and this can prevent the development of more productive strategies for engaging with past trauma. These changes seem to unfold through interactions between the amygdalar processes we discussed above and hippocampal processes that support intrusive thoughts and other cognitive difficulties (Yehuda 2002). Simplifying, memories of traumatic experiences evoke cascades of thoughts about traumatic events, and since they do so in the context of hyperarousal, they tend to support a stable and

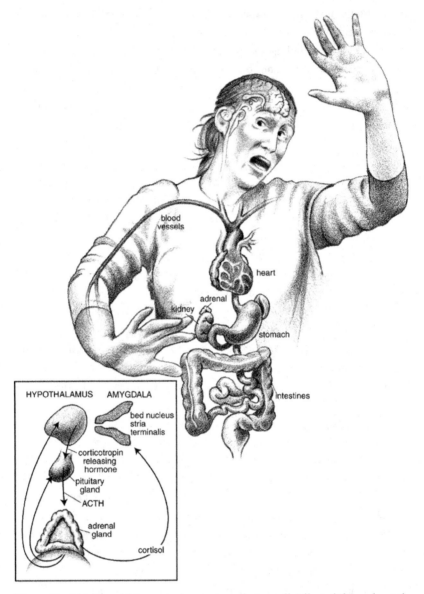

Figure 9 Activity within several processes that are distributed throughout the brain and body are operative in tracking and responding to stressors, threats, and challenges to viability. The inset shows the hypothalamic–pituitary–adrenal axis, the adrenocorticotropic hormone (ACTH) signal, and the amygdala and bed nucleus of the stria terminalis, which all work together to sustain responses to stressors, threats, and challenges to viability.
Image courtesy of John Yansen.

pervasive shift in regulatory processing, yielding pathological states that are incredibly hard to shake.

Fortunately, since numerous interacting systems are calibrated by ongoing social demands, there are multiple ways of managing challenges and opportunities, even where pathological states become deeply entrenched. Put somewhat differently, these processes can be adjusted in different ways to manage salient challenges, and there will often be many ways of adjusting the balance between different sources of information to yield changes in behavior, cognition, and experience. For example, increased levels of oxytocin can increase the willingness to accept social support, gradually diminishing experiences of trauma in PTSD (Heinrichs et al. 2003). The administration of oxytocin can also dampen the reactivity to emotional faces, mitigating the harms of PTSD (Koch et al. 2016). Furthermore, traumatic stimuli can be reconceptualized, traumatic experiences can be de-reified, and feelings of kindness and compassion toward the self and others can be cultivated, and these strategies can help to mitigate the feelings of distress that perpetuate traumatic experiences while also minimizing the lasting effects of trauma (Boyd et al. 2018). Finally, patterns of active social engagement can facilitate the amelioration of social conflict, and more secure forms of social intimacy can be constructed through the social sharing of stories, which can buffer against future social distress (Silver & Sabini 2012). Put bluntly, ongoing regulation is often deeply social. Perhaps this is unsurprising, but it's deeply important if we want to understand human cognition.

4 Social Living

Humans are more helpful, generous, and social than any other ape (Tomasello 2009). We live in highly differentiated groups with high levels of specialization and substantial patterns of trade and exchange. We care for people who are sick, injured, and elderly; we cooperate in ways that stretch beyond the boundaries of our immediate social groups; we share information by pointing, speaking, writing, and teaching – and we do so with people who are neither kith nor kin. Finally, we actively provide aid to others – sometimes dedicating time and resources to assist people we've never met. Rudimentary forms of prosocial behavior emerge early and reliably in human infancy, suggesting that there may be distinctive constraints on human social cognition (Hamlin 2013). By eighteen months of age, infants begin to correct other people's obvious mistakes, and they begin to provide help when objects are out of reach or where there are easily moveable obstacles (Warneken & Tomasello 2006); neither rewards nor encouragement have a noticeable effect on these forms of helping behavior (Warneken et al. 2007). Finally, by age three, children begin to display tendencies to protest, criticize, and intervene against people who have violated social norms (Rakoczy & Schmidt 2013).

The physiological changes that are produced by domestication can shape various social, affective, and cognitive tendencies. Domesticated cats can learn to make demands of their caregivers, and caregivers will often organize their behavior around providing social and nutritional support to their feline companions. As a result, some cats appear to be able to learn how names are associated with human or feline faces (Takagi et al. 2022). More strikingly, domesticated dogs possess rudimentary capacities for cooperative communication – including a responsiveness to human gestures that goes beyond what is commonly observed among nonhuman primates (Hare 2017). However, they also lack many of the other social and affective tendencies that are commonly observed among modern humans (Hare & Tomasello 2005). Finally, most primates possess capacities for managing social alliances, eliciting assistance, and finding workable strategies to ameliorate social and ecological distress (Sapolsky 2005; Wittig et al. 2008). But no nonhuman primate displays the rich array of social and affective capacities that are indicative of human ways of life, and it is unlikely that this is simply a matter of inhabiting different kinds of social worlds.

In fact, the heightened social dependence among members of our species is not a panacea. Social dependence yields numerous opportunities for the pursuit of flourishing. But it also serves as the foundation for pervasive social problems that make it difficult for people who are exposed to persisting social and material distress to flourish. The concept 'allostasis' was introduced to clarify the impact of pervasive social challenges (Sterling & Eyer 1988). Moreover, subsequent approaches to allostasis have emphasized the kind of 'allostatic overload' that often unfolds in the context of pathological stress, as well as the social nature of fear and anticipatory angst (McEwen 1998; Rosen & Schulkin 2004). This is significant, as the uniqueness of human ways of life shapes both what it means for things to go well and what it means for maladaptive strategies to become persistent and stable, and, just as importantly, these connections reveal the pervasive significance of human ecologies that provide numerous opportunities for social learning.

Appeals to these ecologies cannot be the whole story. The rats, bats, and racoons who inhabit urban environments tend to be highly responsive to human behavior (Ritzel & Gallo 2020), but they do not display the robust social tendencies that are commonly observed among humans. The important thing to notice here is that the socio-affective profile that is commonly observed in humans goes far beyond a simple capacity to learn from social feedback. It also goes far beyond what should be expected by a simple process of domestication.

It is likely that constraints on human social cognition have been internalized over evolutionary timescales, and understanding such constraints helps to explain why distinctively human forms of social cognition emerge early and reliably in infancy. But just as importantly, these tendencies are shaped by numerous forms of social feedback, and a more multidimensional approach to *social allostasis* is required to explain how diverse interactions between physiological and social constraints support the development of the wide range of socio-affective profiles that are observed among humans. Crucial features of these interactions are still under investigation, so we will not attempt to provide a complete story about human social cognition, but there is still quite a bit to say about how evolutionary and developmental constraints organize the socio-affective profiles that are observed in modern humans.

4.1 Social and Evolutionary Constraints

In building our case, it will help to begin by considering a common explanation of the social and cognitive capacities of modern dogs. Social tendencies are observed among all canines, but the fact that dogs are more sensitive to human communication reflects a long history of interactions with humans and a multistage process of domestication (Hare et al. 2012, 573). According to the standard story, some canids gained access to new sources of food, including human waste, because they were less fearful and less aggressive around humans; humans also behaved more favorably toward canids who were less skittish and aggressive. Therefore, there were strong selection pressures on the regulation of reactive fear and aggression in canids. Over time, this supported the entrenchment of changes in the chemical signaling systems (oxytocin, corticotropin-releasing hormone, serotonin, testosterone) that are involved in social- and self-regulation (Hare 2017, 165), and the resulting changes to the oxytocin system appear to support an increased willingness to make eye contact, yielding richer capacities for social learning in at least some domesticated dogs (Nagasawa et al. 2015).

Of course, humans are not dogs. But early hominids were probably social animals who lived in small multifamily communities that were governed by linear dominance hierarchies. Shifts in climate and habitat forced these hominids to scavenge on open grasslands in search of novel food resources (Tomasello et al. 2012, 676). In general, apes will travel and forage together if doing so reduces predation risk, but if these apes found new sources of food (maybe bone marrow or tubers), and if traveling together became commonplace, this would yield more than an increase in security and a decrease in predation risk. It would also yield improved access to food and mates, which might provide an initial nudge toward more richly textured social lives (Clutton-Brock 2009).

The ability to adapt *with others* seems to have been a distinctive feature of the hominid lineage across numerous timescales. As different hominids migrated into diverse ecological contexts, they needed to form stable coalitions while learning to track changes in the conditions for preserving individual and social stability (Silk 2007; Silk et al. 2013). In this context, we should expect the increases in cortical volume that are observed across human evolution (Byrne & Whiten 1988; Dunbar 2016). Cortical volume tends to increase where social life becomes more complex, across numerous different contexts such as social play, tactical deception, and coalition formation (Reader & Laland 2002). But large brains are metabolically costly, and improved access to energy-rich foods, as well as changes in capacities to metabolize calories, are necessary to preserve them. In this context, part of the work in supporting large brains could have been done by learning to hunt and forage collectively and improving access to calories through cooking (Wrangham 2019). But just as importantly, improvements in hunting, foraging, and cooking would have been scaffolded by a diverse range of social skills, such as toolmaking. These capacities would require heightened sensitivities to opportunities to teach and learn, and they would have required heightened sensitivities to social pressure and social status (Gweon 2021; Sykes 2020). Therefore, a plausible story about the evolution of human cognition has to be understood as a story about the evolution of human social cognition. But this is also where we need a slight shift in focus.

As they learned to survive and flourish *together* in complex and dangerous environments, hominids would have become more attentive to social demands and social information. Moreover, learning to live *collectively* would have favored increases in impulse control and perhaps longer windows of socialization, while diminishing patterns of fear and reactive aggression (Wrangham 2019). There are ongoing disputes about the cause of these changes, and we will not attempt to settle them here (compare Shilton et al. 2020; Sterelny 2021; Wilkins et al. 2014), but there is broad agreement that the effects of these processes, whatever they might be, are observable in the context of human development. Some of these effects parallel the ones that we discussed in dogs, yielding opportunities for lower-stress interactions with others early in life. But increased opportunities for social learning have more substantial effects in large-brained primates who are prepared to learn how to live with others. Most importantly, being prepared to learn how to live socially allows interactions with caregivers to play numerous different roles in shaping developmental pathways, which can lead to an increased willingness to engage in complex social interactions later in life. We want to be clear: These developmental pathways are supported by diverse capacities for the regulation of social affect, and not just the diminishment of reactive stress or increases in impulse control. To see what this means, we need to look more carefully at some of the interactions between chemical signaling systems and social contexts that support typical human sociality (Fam et al. 2018; Hare 2017). Specifically, we need to consider the possibility that early interactions between infants and caretakers support the development of richly textured forms of human sociality (Hrdy 2011).

There is a rapidly expanding consensus that diverse forms of learning are organized by the demands of allostatic regulation. As Shir Atzil and her colleagues (2018) argue, social cognition develops as processes that target the sensory consequences of allostasis are calibrated against social regularities. To explain how this process of calibration occurs, Atzil and her colleagues focus on early interactions with caregivers, and they argue that infants employ Bayesian learning mechanisms to construct a model of who provides them with access to food and other resources. This kind of learning might play a role in the development of social cognition. But we contend that a more diverse range of regulatory processes are calibrated, using a more diverse range of feedback relations, as infants learn to rely upon caretakers.

4.2 Chemical Signals and Sociality

To begin with, consider the interactions that are supported by the oxytocin system. Oxytocin is a chemical signal that acts in a multitude of ways throughout the nervous system (Carter 2017; Insel 1992; Power & Schulkin 2017; Quintana & Guastella 2020). Oxytocin is not *just* a social molecule. Like all chemical messengers, it is used differently in different contexts to dynamically modify neural activity. It can affect decisions to approach or avoid situations. It plays numerous important roles in gestation, birth, and lactation. It also modulates food intake and gastric motility. But it also shapes the ways that mothers respond to stressors and infant demands, it organizes interactions between mothers and their infant children by supporting infant-directed eye gaze and shifting patterns of vocalization and expressions of positive affect, and it can even modulate the willingness of male parents and alloparents to engage in nurturing behavior.

In adults, differences in the availability of oxytocin can shape the direction and magnitude of caring and concerned affect. They can also shape tendencies to support those who are perceived as close social others or safe social partners. Indeed, increases in available oxytocin can even promote prosocial behavior in people with lower levels of baseline trust, at least where they feel like an interaction will be safe. But differences in the availability of oxytocin are not a panacea. The increased availability of oxytocin can also evoke aversion toward outgroup members and promote in-group favoritism, and it can even decrease trust and prosociality in people with borderline personality disorder (Marsh et al. 2021). So, any story about the social significance of oxytocin must be integrated into a broader story about the effects of every other process that is operating as someone attempts to navigate social challenges and opportunities. For our purposes, however, it is important to note that differences in maternal caregiving are often supported by differences in the oxytocin system (Churchland 2019; Marsh 2016, 64–65), and these differences support a dense feedback loop that links diverse regulatory phenomena to the tolerance of social stress and the receipt of social support.

On the one hand, specific social contexts – including breastfeeding, coordinated interactions, and physical contact – tend to promote the release of oxytocin. This can yield a diminished reactivity to fearful expressions, as well as increased attention to infant faces and increased motivations to approach fear expressions (Marsh et al. 2012). These tendencies might provide the foundation for compassionate action, which aims to mitigate the effects of social stress. On the other hand, once oxytocin is released, it can regulate diverse forms of social cognition and social behavior. Intriguingly, higher levels of parental involvement seem to have an effect on the regulation of oxytocin receptor genes, which supports a more balanced emotional temperament in response to expressions of anger and fear, though these effects are dynamic and sensitive to features of the local social environment (Krol et al. 2019a, 2019b). Over time, this interactive process appears to shape attachment styles, yielding substantial long-term effects on cognition and behavior. For example, differences in neural and attentional responses to fearful faces at seven months predict differences in prosocial behavior at fourteen months (Grossmann et al. 2018). These differences affect how infants attend to social information, how they represent social relationships, and whether they will seek social support to regulate stress (Chen et al. 2011, 2017).

The existing developmental data also suggest that expecting reliable and secure social support allows infants to use social interactions to mitigate social and ecological distress (Gunnar 2017). Interactions with caregivers play crucial roles in the development of these kinds of cognitive and behavioral profiles by calibrating expectations about social support and tendencies toward social wariness (Raglan et al. 2017). The provision of social support is shaped by the chemical signaling of oxytocin, while tendencies to experience social wariness are shaped by the chemical signaling of corticotropin-releasing hormone. Similar effects persist throughout life: In the context of mature friendships and romantic relationships, security and stability can buffer against the effects of stress, and they can minimize mental and physical discomfort – though, critically, such effects appear to differ as a function of gendered expectations, attachment style, and patterns of anticipated support from others (Eisenberg et al. 2017; Powers et al. 2006). But if infants learn that others can help them to regulate social stress, and if they come to perceive others as sources of cooperation and coordination, this can open up space for more robust forms of social learning and social dependence.

Diverse forms of social contact with caregivers play prominent roles in development, and they are all shaped by different neural and chemical processes. We cannot discuss all of these factors here. But as we noted in Section 3.4, there are many chemical signals (such as glucocorticoids, corticotropin-releasing hormone, vasopressin) that play significant roles in the development and regulation of strategies for managing challenges and opportunities. Such chemical signals are often produced in anticipation of facing a specific challenge or opportunity, and they initiate the diverse kinds of physiological, behavioral, and cognitive processes that will be required to manage perceived stressors, threats, and challenges to viability. Such effects play a prominent role in shaping sociality over the course of development, and there is evidence that anticipated support from a caregiver can often buffer against the effects of social and ecological distress. For example, developmental studies consistently reveal that while infants and caretakers are visibly distressed by being separated – even briefly – this distress does not appear to evoke the predicted cascade of activity along the hypothalamic–pituitary–adrenal axis if they are rapidly reunited (Gunnar 2017).

Beyond these kinds of effects, infants must also learn when and where food is likely to be available, and they must learn who can be trusted to satisfy nutritional needs. This occurs in a context where caretakers are scaffolding the transition from a single digestible food to a diet consisting of numerous different foods. But this is far from the end of the story. Over the course of development, infants must acquire sensitivities to numerous sources of information about what others are eating. Early in life, their preferences tend to shift toward the food preferences of people with familiar accents (Shutts et al. 2013). By the age of six, children begin to track the food preferences of other children (DeJesus et al. 2018b). Moreover, while they continue to observe what their caretakers eat, children grow increasingly insensitive to what caretakers say about the foods they eat over the course of development (DeJesus et al. 2018a). Just as importantly, children adjust their food preferences to bring them into alignment with relevant forms of group identification, accommodating numerous social interactions that cluster around practices of eating together (Hackel et al. 2018). In each of these contexts, food preferences are shaped by diverse bodily, neural, chemical, and social constraints.

Finally, patterns of affect-biased attention appear to be socially shaped over the course of development. Put somewhat differently, infants seem to learn that stimuli are salient through interactions with caregivers, which are in turn shaped by feelings of social dependence. Evidence supporting these claims comes from a recent study, which found: (1) higher levels of self-reported maternal anxiety tended to correlate with a reduction in how much time infants would spend engaging with emotionally salient faces; but (2) infants who had a more negative emotional temperament, and parents with higher levels of anxiety, tended to have a more vigilant attentional profile – that is, these infants oriented toward emotional faces more rapidly and dedicated greater attention resources to such faces (Vallorani et al. 2021). These forms of attentional prioritization are the same kinds of processes that we discussed in Section 2.4. But in a developmental context, where children are learning how to regulate social stress, they can yield lasting and pervasive effects on the ways that people will engage in social interactions later in life.

Collectively, these phenomena point toward a more general fact about social development that goes beyond the ways that infants calibrate interoceptive signals against social feedback: Social attachment and social engagement are dynamically regulated through complex interactions between physiological differences, early engagement with caregivers, and ongoing patterns of social feedback and social categorization. Social cognition is a massively complex affair that is supported and organized by numerous different patterns of allostatic co-regulation; indeed, this must be the case, as social contexts are always ripe with multiple forms of ambiguity. From this perspective, it becomes clear that development is not simply a matter of learning what the world is like; it is a process of learning whom to trust, when to explore new situations, when to be wary of strangers, and how to respond to countless other social and ecological phenomena. When affective tendencies are coupled to differences in access to food and other resources, a complex and multidimensional picture of human sociality comes into view. This makes social cognition messy and complex, and it yields numerous pattens of diversity in the calibration of different systems. But this is how things should be from a biological point of view. After all, infants must learn about diverse challenges and opportunities, and numerous bodily and neural systems must be calibrated over the course of development. There should be no doubt that evolutionary and developmental constraints, along with diverse forms of learning, are operative in learning to navigate challenges and opportunities (Schulkin 2011), but does a plausible account of these processes really need to be as complex and multidimensional as we have suggested?

5 Complex Trade-Offs and Higher Cognition

Research in computational neuroscience is beginning to acknowledge that an understanding of allostatic regulation is necessary if we are to explain cognition and behavior (Allen & Tsakiris 2018; Corcoran & Hohwy 2019). Such approaches often treat cognitive processes as metabolic investments that use energy in the form of glucose and glycogen, and they commonly claim that centrally located neural networks monitor physiological states and adjust processing to manage crucial bodily variables (Barrett & Simmons 2015). To the extent that the 'acceptable range' of a physiological variable can be specified as the state of a computational model, deviations from this acceptable range can be understood as error signals that demand correction (Theriault et al. 2021, 106), and, on the assumption that the brain constructs a model of the likely cause of its bodily and perceptual states, this model can be adjusted to minimize the threats to viability that error signals would seem to represent (Tschantz et al. 2021). Anil Seth (2021) has articulated a plausible version of this hypothesis, where active measures are taken to bring an essential variable (such as blood glucose) within an acceptable range whenever it threatens to fall below an established threshold. From this perspective, deviations from acceptable values are coded as prediction errors, which evoke top-down expectations that are experienced as thirst or hunger. Since such experiences are nonviable in the long run, they tend to trigger cascades of activity that can be resolved either by metabolizing fat stores or by finding and eating sugary things.

The arguments that we have developed in this Element suggest that Seth's approach points in a promising direction, but we doubt that it will be possible to capture the complexity of the neural and chemical systems that support allostatic regulation within a story about computations and error signals. After all, animals must routinely manage numerous trade-offs between exploring environments and finding efficient ways to exploit available resources, and numerous chemical messengers, as well as multiple forms of physiological and social feedback, must be employed to preserve viability in a complex environment. More progress is likely to be made by focusing on the diverse roles that are played by physical, chemical, and social constraints. No doubt, energy regulation is one important feature that must be taken into account in explaining how bodily, neural, and chemical systems support cognition. But the complexity of physiological regulation shapes cognition in profound ways.

Neural and chemical systems operate over multiple timescales to sustain thought and behavior, and *biological cognition* is often a juggling act that reflects ongoing attempts to minimize disruptions while prioritizing challenges and opportunities. As Peter Sterling and Joseph Eyer (1988) note, social disruptions – including war, migration, segregation, unemployment, and racial strife – tend to increase the rate of hypertension, stroke, and heart disease. Sterling and Eyer's initial discussion of allostatic regulation highlighted the impact of disruptions of social relations on capacities to navigate opportunities and challenges within the social milieu, and they argued that the activity in the diverse bodily systems that are recruited to manage physiological and social challenges often come to reflect the features of the world where a person lives and acts. Subsequent discussions of allostatic regulation highlighted the neural and chemical processes that produce fear and anxiety in response to dangers, and this led to the hypothesis that sustained and chronic activity in these systems could produce forms of hyperexcitability that would yield persisting forms of stress and anxiety (Rosen & Schulkin 2004). Finally, Bruce McEwen (1998) argued that the effects of social conflict and social disharmony are often manifested physiologically, as increases in *social allostatic load* that must be managed and minimized by social animals. But even this should not be seen as the end of the story.

The same neural and chemical processes will often have several different uses. Moreover, trade-offs between these partially overlapping processes will often be regulated by chemical messengers that organize embodied patterns of adaptive coping. Across these neural and chemical systems, there is evidence of learning-dependent plasticity, especially in stressful contexts and contexts where challenges must be faced to preserve viability. For example, gene expression is frequently regulated in response to novel and stressful situations (McEwen 2017), and epigenetic effects can produce continuous patterns of changes in neural tissue and circuitry. Such changes help animals to respond to challenges, and they can also support resilience and adaptability through changing circumstances. Consider the way that the network structure of the amygdala and hippocampus can be transformed in response to threats and distress. On the one hand, chemical signals can promote structural and functional changes to neural organization in structures like the hippocampus, amygdalar complex, and basal ganglia as a response to ongoing stress and chronic social defeat (Fox et al. 2020). On the other hand, chronic stress can also increase the volume of the amygdala, while decreasing the volume of the hippocampus (Chattarji et al. 2015; Vyas et al. 2002). These kinds of effects prepare animals to confront challenges, but they can also support lasting forms of anxiety and distress that become difficult to dislodge. These effects are vital for learning and memory, but they are difficult to situate within many of the functionalist and computational frameworks that have dominated research in the cognitive sciences. The key problem here is that the parts and processes that are relevant to explaining thought and behavior change in ways that are sensitive to the demand of preserving viability across changing circumstances. In this context, failing to find obvious correlations between neural activity and patterns of thought and behavior shouldn't lead us to abandon the search for distributed and flexible networks that can sustain adaptive behavior without centralized regulation (Brezina 2010). It should lead us to think differently about these kinds of phenomena.

5.1 'Higher' Cognition?

This brings us to the elephant in the room. What should this approach to biological cognition say about so-called 'higher' capacities such as belief, logical reasoning, and the acquisition and use of language? The short answer is, we are not sure. But we suggest that such questions should be reframed in ways that highlight the significance of physiological, social, and ecological constraints. We also suggest that familiar forms of functionalism, as well as simplified appeals to computations and representations, should be supplemented with a recognition that adjustments will often be made in one system to compensate for adjustments that have been made in others, and it should be acknowledged that neural processing is often widely distributed, shaped in complex ways by chemical messengers, and organized by diverse components that change in response to physiological, social, and ecological demands.

The key insight is that 'higher cognition' will typically reflect complex interactions between networks of evolved, developmental, and physiological constraints that collectively shape learning and social engagement. Perhaps this is unsurprising. Many adults appear to be primarily concerned with the avoidance of psychological discomfort and the minimization of cognitive dissonance. This might be part of the reason why many adults display robust patterns of belief perseverance, as well as group-based belief polarization, and tendencies to increase their credence in identity-preserving claims despite acknowledging the existence of disconfirming evidence (Mandelbaum 2019). But this drive to avoid stress and discomfort can manifest in really striking ways. For example, psychosomatic disorders might help people to avoid reexperiencing predicted traumas, while preserving their identities and core assumptions about how the world works (O'Sullivan 2017). Each of these phenomena remind us that humans are highly social, embodied, and actively engaged animals who must develop strategies to make sense of the world as they find it. This is the basis for the kind of embodied pluralism that we have developed throughout this Element, but it cuts all the way through human cognition, perhaps most strikingly in the context of the acquisition and use of language.

In closing, we would thus like to consider the capacities that must be in place for a child to acquire and use a language. In the case of auditory language, there appear to be two processing streams: one appears to track fast temporal variations, which are associated with phonetic structure; the other appears to track slower patterns of variation, which are associated with different speakers. By six months of gestation, preterm infants already display an enhanced capacity to discriminate different phonemes (for example, /ba/ vs /ga/), relative to their capacity to discriminate different voices (Dehaene-Lambertz 2017), and by three months of age, different patterns of neural activity in the first stream begin to track differences in manner (obstruent; sonorant) and place of articulation (labial; alveolar; velar), before reintegrating these features to track higher-level phonemic regularities (Gennari et al. 2021). Such processes appear to play a critical role in organizing the flow of auditory information into useable linguistic structures.

Things become substantially more complicated in the context of learning syntax and morphology. In these contexts, statistical learning processes appear to play a critical role in language acquisition, but the kinds of regularities that children learn are highly constrained. On the one hand, syntactic and morphological regularities display a Zipfian distribution – that is, the probability of the occurrence of a syntactic or morphological feature tends to be inversely proportional to its rank in a frequency table. On the other hand, humans seem to be biologically prepared to track such distributions, using a simple rule-extraction process to recover structured patterns from noisy linguistic data (Yang 2016).

Where linguistic input is noisy or irregular, children display patterns of statistical sharpening and regularization that bring them into alignment with the structures and rules that organize the language they are learning (Newport 2016). This is perhaps clearest in contexts where a child must learn a sign language from parents who learned this language later in life, without access to a broader community of native signers. Like late learners of other languages, parents who learn a sign language later in life make frequent mistakes and use complex constructions inconsistently. But when children acquire a sign language by interacting with late learners, they tend to ignore these errors, and as a result they produce morphemes and sentences that are more regular and more consistent with the standard constructions in the language they are learning.

There is little consensus about how such learning capacities are implemented. However, one recent hypothesis suggests that language acquisition and use employs processes of neural inhibition and gain modulation across numerous distributed processes to track hierarchically structured patterns (Martin 2020). Critically, these forms of pattern tracking do not seem to be tied to specific sensory modalities (such as sight, hearing, or touch). Deaf children who acquire a sign language and hearing children who acquire a spoken language achieve the same developmental milestones at approximately the same time. Furthermore, acquiring a sign language early in life facilitates learning a spoken language later in life, and acquiring a spoken language early in life facilitates learning a sign language later in life (Mayberry & Kluender 2018, 893).

That said, there is evidence that the hierarchical structure of language and the structure of the neural systems that process linguistic information are shaped by interactions between social and maturational constraints. This becomes clearest in the context of Deaf children who are raised within hearing families, and who encounter sign languages later in life. Deaf children must employ numerous workarounds to navigate the challenges and opportunities of interacting with hearing family members. Sometimes, they will develop homesign systems that display patterns of word ordering and other linguistic structures that are never observed in the gestures of their family members (Goldin-Meadow 2005). This is commonly taken to be evidence that some aspects of first-language acquisition are resilient to variations in learning environments; specifically, it is often suggested that children are able to produce rule-governed structures even though they never encounter them. But we should proceed cautiously. Homesign systems do not seem to facilitate the latter acquisition of other languages (Mayberry & Kluender 2018, 895), and understanding why this is the case requires thinking carefully about developmental constraints on the acquisition of a first language.

Many Deaf children who are born to hearing parents begin to learn a sign language later in life. Where a first language is acquired around the age of six, children quickly develop the ability to use two-word constructions, and they tend to develop a working understanding of stable word-order. This yields a shift from gesturing to signing. However, they continue to struggle with tasks that require matching sentences to pictures or describing scenes, and they continue to make phonological errors. The acquisition of a first language during adolescence has even more profound effects. These later learners rapidly acquire vocabulary items, as well as two-word constructions and simple word-order constraints. However, they struggle to produce or understand complex morphological, syntactic, and phonological structures, and they do so even after substantial language instruction and immersion in linguistic communities who use the language (Mayberry & Kluender 2018, 896). These difficulties appear to be localized to linguistic *structure building*. Later learners might be familiar with a large number of signs, they might be able to engage in sophisticated patterns of reasoning, and they will often be able to produce communicative constructions with a basic word-order, but they will struggle with complex verb morphology, they will find it difficult to rearrange signs while maintaining the overall meaning of a sentence, and they will produce bare stems that are stripped of any inflectional morphology. Perhaps most strikingly, this will remain true even after as many as thirty years of using the language!

In typical contexts, patterns of increasing specialization in the processing of linguistic structures are commonly observed over the course of development. These include patterns of lateralization, as well as the stabilization of language-relevant processing in regions of the frontal lobe. But importantly, these patterns are not observed as clearly in people who acquire their first language later in life. Later learners appear to rely more heavily on processes in the visual cortex, and when they watch someone signing, they display patterns of neural activity that are more similar to watching meaningless actions than to processing a language (Mayberry & Kluender 2018, 899). It would be easy to read this as a deficit, but from our perspective what we see here is a person who has learned to deal with the kinds of challenges and opportunities that were available to them early in life. Rather than dedicating resources to tracking complex linguistic structures, later learners develop capacities to attend to the visual phenomena they can use to navigate the situations that they encounter, and for a Deaf person who must navigate a hearing world without using a language, it makes more sense to attend to visual particularities rather than linguistic generalities.

Finally, and perhaps most importantly, interactions between Deaf children can transform homesign systems into more robust, stable, and shared languages that suit the needs of a specific community (Brentari & Goldin-Meadow 2017). This process happens from the bottom up, and it can take multiple generations for the processes of regularization, rule learning, and ongoing feedback to develop the kinds of complexities that we commonly encounter in language. But crucially, this suggests that interactions with others, and attempts to make sense of one another, are likely to play an integral role in the development of language. That said, many of the processes that support language acquisition are resilient across changes to sensory input; in fact, they don't even need to be tied to auditory or visual information. For example, a DeafBlind community has recently started to develop a linguistic system that relies on tactile interactions, with patterns of touch and proprioceptive monitoring encoding formal linguistic categories where hearing and vision are unavailable (Edwards & Brentari 2020).

The key thing to notice across these contexts is that the early acquisition of a language supports robust capacities for tracking amodal patterns that are invariant across sensory experiences. Perhaps this is an instance of a more general fact about structure learning: Young children explore a wider range of possibilities, and they learn precise rules even when they are exposed to noisy sources of information. By contrast, adults who would be able to track statistical regularities if they were trying to do so often rely on assumptions about which rules must be in play, and this can lead them to miss the statistical patterns that children reliably discover (Gopnik et al. 2017; Newport 2020). Understanding why this is the case requires a careful examination of the interactions between social context, maturational constraints, and the kinds of challenges and opportunities that must be navigated at various points in development (Newport 1988). There is a great deal more work that must be done in spelling out this approach, but we hope that this Element can serve as a first step along the path of getting diverse researchers to think together about these issues, and we hope that our arguments reveal new ways of working together to attain a kind of predictive coherence among the diverse strategies that are currently employed in trying to understand *biological cognition*.

References

Abramson, C. I. (2009). A study in inspiration: Charles Henry Turner (1867–1923) and the investigation of insect behavior. *Annual Review of Entomology*, 54, 343–359.

Allen, C. (2017). On (not) defining cognition. *Synthese*, 194(11), 4233–4249.

Allen, M., & Tsakiris, M. (2018). The body as first prior: Interoceptive predictive processing and the primacy. *The interoceptive mind: From homeostasis to awareness* (pp. 27–45). Oxford University Press.

Anderson, B. (2016). The attention habit: How reward learning shapes attentional selection. *Annals of New York Academy Sciences*, 1369(1), 24–39.

Anderson, M. L. (2014). *After phrenology: Neural reuse and the interactive brain*. MIT Press.

Anderson, M. L. (2015). Beyond componential constitution in the brain – Starburst amacrine cells and enabling constraints. In T. Metzinger & J. M. Windt (Eds.), *Open MIND*: 1(T). MIND Group. https://bit.ly/3Tfo1Cv.

Anderson, M. L., & Chemero, A. (2019). *The world well gained: Andy Clark and his critics*. Oxford University Press.

Archie, E. A., Moss, C. J., & Alberts, S. C. (2011). Friends and relations: Kinship and the nature of female elephant social relationships. In C. Moss, H. Croze, & P. C. Lee (Eds.), *The Amboseli elephants: A long-term perspective on a long-lived mammal* (pp. 238–245). University of Chicago Press.

Atzil, S., Gao, W., Fradkin, I., & Barrett, L. F. (2018). Growing a social brain. *Nature Human Behaviour*, 2(9), 624–636.

Baccus, S. A., & Meister, M. (2002). Fast and slow contrast adaptation in retinal circuitry. *Neuron*, 36(5), 909–919.

Baden, T., Euler, T., & Berens, P. (2020). Understanding the retinal basis of vision across species. *Nature Reviews Neuroscience*, 21(1), 5–20.

Barlow, H. B. (1972). Single units and sensation: A neuron doctrine for perceptual psychology? *Perception*, 1(4), 371–394.

Barrett, L. F. (2017). *How emotions are made: The secret life of the brain*. Houghton Mifflin Harcourt.

Barrett, L. F., & Simmons, W. K. (2015). Interoceptive predictions in the brain. *Nature Reviews Neuroscience*, 16(7), 419–429.

Barwich, A. S. (2019). A critique of olfactory objects. *Frontiers in Psychology*, 10, 1337.

Bates, L. A., Poole, J. H., & Byrne, R. W. (2008). Elephant cognition. *Current Biology*, 18(13), R544–R546.

Baumgartner, H. M., Schulkin, J., & Berridge, K. C. (2021). Activating corticotropin releasing factor (CRF) systems in nucleus accumbens, amygdala, and bed nucleus of stria terminalis: Incentive motivation or aversive motivation? *Biological Psychiatry*, 89, 1162–1175.

Bechtel, W. (2009). Looking down, around, and up: Mechanistic explanation in psychology. *Philosophical Psychology*, 22(5), 543–564.

Bechtel, W., & Huang, L. (2022). *The philosophy of neuroscience*. Cambridge University Press.

Bernard, C. (1974). *Lectures on the phenomena of life common to animals and plants* (Vol. 2, No. 1). Charles C Thomas Pub.

Berridge, K. C. (2012). From prediction error to incentive salience: Mesolimbic computation of reward motivation. *European Journal of Neuroscience*, 35(7), 1124–1143.

Berridge, K. C., Flynn, F. W., Schulkin, J., & Grill, H. J. (1984). Sodium depletion enhances salt palatability in rats. *Behavioral Neuroscience*, 98(4), 652–660.

Berridge, K. C., Grill, H. J., & Norgren, R. (1981). Relation of consummatory responses and preabsorptive insulin release to palatability and learned taste aversions. *Journal of Comparative and Physiological Psychology*, 95(3), 363–382.

Berridge, K. C., & Schulkin, J. (1989). Palatability shift of a salt-associated incentive during sodium depletion. *The Quarterly Journal of Experimental Psychology*, 41(2), 121–138.

Bizley, J. K., & Cohen, Y. E. (2013). The what, where and how of auditory-object perception. *Nature Reviews Neuroscience*, 14(10), 693–707.

Blair-West, J. R., Coghlan, J. P., Denton, D. A. et al. (1968). Physiological, morphological and behavioural adaptation to a sodium deficient environment by wild native Australian and introduced species of animals. *Nature*, 217(5132), 922–928.

Blakemore, C., & Campbell, F. W. (1969). On the existence of neurons in the human visual system selectively sensitive to the orientation and size of retinal images. *The Journal of Physiology*, 203(1), 237–260.

Boyd, J. E., Lanius, R. A., & McKinnon, M. C. (2018). Mindfulness-based treatments for posttraumatic stress disorder. *Journal of Psychiatry & Neuroscience*, 43(1), 7–25.

Bradshaw, G. A. (2009). *Elephants on the edge*. Yale University Press.

Bradshaw, G. A., & Schore, A. N. (2007). How elephants are opening doors: Developmental neuroethology, attachment and social context. *Ethology*, 113(5), 426–436.

Brentari, D., & Goldin-Meadow, S. (2017). Language emergence. *The Annual Review of Linguistics*, 3, 363–388.

Brezina, V. (2010). Beyond the wiring diagram: Signaling through complex neuromodulator networks. *Philosophical Transactions of the Royal Society B: Biological Sciences*, 365(1551), 2363–2374.

Brown, R., Brusse, C., Huebner, B., & Pain, R. (2020). Unification at the cost of realism and precision. *Behavioral and Brian Sciences*, 43.

Buckner, C. (2018). Empiricism without magic: Transformational abstraction in deep convolutional neural networks. *Synthese*, 195(12), 5339–5372.

Buzsáki, G. (2019). *The brain from inside out.* Oxford University Press.

Byrne, R. W., & Whiten, A. (1988). *Machiavellian intelligence: Social expertise and the evolution of intellect in monkeys, apes, and humans.* Clarendon.

Campbell, F. W., & Maffei, L. (1974). Contrast and spatial frequency. *Scientific American*, 231(5), 106–115.

Cannon, W. B. (1917). *Bodily changes in pain, hunger, fear, and rage: An account of recent researches into the function of emotional excitement.* D. Appleton.

Cannon, W. B. (1932). *The wisdom of the body.* W. W. Norton. Carandini, M., Demb, J. B., Mante, V. et al. (2005). Do we know what the early visual system does? *Journal of Neuroscience*, 25(46), 10577–10597.

Carter, C. S. (2017). The oxytocin–vasopressin pathway in the context of love and fear. *Frontiers in Endocrinology*, 8, 356.

Carrasco, M. (2011). Visual attention: The past 25 years. *Vision Research*, 51(13), 1484–1525.

Chattarji, S., Tomar, A., Suvrathan, A., Ghosh, S., & Rahman, M. M. (2015). Neighborhood matters: Divergent patterns of stress-induced plasticity across the brain. *Nature Neuroscience*, 18(10), 1364–1375.

Chen, F. S., Barth, M., Johnson, SL., Gotlib, I. H., & Johnson, S. C. (2011). Oxytocin receptor (OXTR) polymorphisms and attachment in human infants. *Frontiers in Psychology*, 2, 200.

Chen, F. S., Heinrichs, M., & Johnson, S. C. (2017). Oxytocin and the emergence of individual differences in the social regulation of stress. *Social and Personality Psychology Compass*, 11(8), e12332.

Churchland, P. S. (2019). *Conscience: The origins of moral intuition.* W. W. Norton & Company.

Clutton-Brock, T. (2009). Cooperation between non-kin in animal societies. *Nature*, 462(7269), 51–57.

Corcoran, A. W., & Hohwy, J. (2019). Allostasis, interoception, and the free energy principle: Feeling our way forward. In M. Tsakiris & H. de Preester

(Eds.), *The interoceptive mind: From homeostasis to awareness* (pp. 272–292). Oxford University Press.

Corlett, P. R., Frith, C. D., & Fletcher, P. C. (2009). From drugs to deprivation. *Psychopharmacology*, 206(4), 515–530.

Corlett, P. R., Horga, G., Fletcher, P. C., Alderson-Day, B., Schmack, K., & Powers, A. R. III (2019). Hallucinations and strong priors. *Trends in Cognitive Sciences*, 23(2), 114–127.

Corris, A. (2020). Defining the environment in organism–environment systems. *Frontiers in Psychology*, 11, 1285.

Cummins, D. D., & Cummins, R. (1999). Biological preparedness and evolutionary explanation. *Cognition*, 73(3), B37–B53.

Dallman, M. F., Strack, A. M., Akana, S. F. et al. (1993). Feast and famine: Critical role of glucocorticoids with insulin in daily energy flow. *Frontiers in Neuroendocrinology*, 14(4), 303–347.

Daniels, D., & Schulkin, J. (2018). Water and salt intake in vertebrates: Endocrine and Behavioral Regulation. In *Encyclopaedia of animal behavior* (pp. 569–579). Academic Press.

Davies-Barton, T., Raja, V., Baggs, E., & Anderson, M. L. (2022). Debt-free intelligence: Ecological information in minds and machines. http://philsci-archive.pitt.edu/20426/.

Davis, M., & Whalen, P. J. (2001). The amygdala: Vigilance and emotion. *Molecular Psychiatry*, 6(1), 13–34.

Dayan, P., & Niv, Y. (2008). Reinforcement learning: The good, the bad and the ugly. *Current Opinion in Neurobiology*, 18(2), 185–196.

Dehaene-Lambertz, G. (2017). The human infant brain: A neural architecture able to learn language. *Psychonomic Bulletin & Review*, 24(1), 48–55.

DeJesus, J. M., Gelman, S. A., Viechnicki, G. B. et al. (2018a). An investigation of maternal food intake and maternal food talk as predictors of child food intake. *Appetite*, 127, 356–363.

DeJesus, J. M., Shutts, K., & Kinzler, K. D. (2018b). Mere social knowledge impacts children's consumption and categorization of foods. *Developmental Science*, 21(5), e12627.

Dennett, D. C. (1995). *Darwin's dangerous idea*. Simon and Schuster.

Denton, D. A. (1982). *Hunger for salt*. Springer-Verlag.

Desimone, R., & Duncan, J. (1995). Neural mechanisms of selective visual attention. *Annual Review of Neuroscience*, 18(1), 193–222.

DiCarlo, J. J., Zoccolan, D., & Rust, N. C. (2012). How does the brain solve visual object recognition? *Neuron*, 73(3), 415–434.

Dunbar, R. (2016). *Human evolution: Our brains and behavior*. Oxford University Press.

Edwards, T., & Brentari, D. (2020). Feeling phonology: The conventionalization of phonology in protactile communities in the United States. *Language*, 96(4), 819–840.

Eisenberger, N. I., Moieni, M., Inagaki, T. K., Muscatell, K. A., & Irwin, M. R. (2017). In sickness and in health: The co-regulation of inflammation and social behavior. *Neuropsychopharmacology*, 42(1), 242–253.

Engel, A., Fries, P., & Singer, W. (2001). Dynamic predictions: Oscillations and synchrony in top–down processing. *Nature Reviews Neuroscience*, 2(10), 704–716.

Epstein, A. N. (1982). Mineralocorticoids and cerebral angiotensin may act together to produce sodium appetite. *Peptides*, 3(3), 493–494.

Ewert, J. P. (1984). Behavioral selectivity based on thalamotectal interactions: Ontogenetic and phylogenetic aspects in amphibians. *Behavioral and Brain Sciences*, 7(3), 337–338.

Ewert, J. P. (1997). Neural correlates of key stimulus and releasing mechanism: A case study and two concepts. *Trends in Neurosciences*, 20(8), 332–339.

Ewert, J.-P., Buxbaum-Conradi, H., Dreisvogt, F. et al. (2001). Neural modulation of visuomotor functions underlying prey-catching behaviour in anurans: Perception, attention, motor performance, learning. *Comparative Biochemistry and Physiology Part A: Molecular & Integrative Physiology*, 128(3), 417–460.

Fam, B. S., Paré, P., Felkl, A. B., et al. (2018). Oxytocin and arginine vasopressin systems in the domestication process. *Genetics and Molecular Biology*, 41(1 suppl 1), 235–242.

Felleman, D. J., & Van Essen, D. C. (1991). Distributed hierarchical processing in the primate cerebral cortex. *Cerebral Cortex*, 1(1), 1–47.

Fitzsimons, J. T. (1979). *The physiology of thirst and sodium appetite*. Monographs of the Physiological Society, 35. Oxford University Press.

Fox, M. E., Figueiredo, A., Menken, M. S., & Lobo, M. K. (2020). Dendritic spine density is increased on nucleus accumbens D2 neurons after chronic social defeat. *Scientific Reports*, 10(1), 1–7.

Freud, E., Plaut, D. C., & Behrmann, M. (2016). 'What' is happening in the dorsal visual pathway. *Trends in Cognitive Sciences*, 20(10), 773–784.

Galef, B. G., & Laland, K. N. (2005). Social learning in animals: Empirical studies and theoretical models. *Bioscience*, 55(6), 489–499.

Gandhi, T., Kalia, A., Ganesh, S., & Sinha, P. (2015). Immediate susceptibility to visual illusions after sight onset. *Current Biology*, 25(9), R358–R359.

Garcia, J., & Koelling, R. A. (1966). Relation of cue to consequence in avoidance learning. *Psychonomic Science*, 4(1), 123–124.

Geerling, J. C., & Loewy, A. D. (2008). Central regulation of sodium appetite. *Experimental Physiology*, 93(2), 177–209.

Gennari, G., Marti, S., Palu, M., Fló, A., & Dehaene-Lambertz, G. (2021). Orthogonal neural codes for speech in the infant brain. *Proceedings of the National Academy of Sciences*, 118(31), e2020410118.

Ghosh, D. D., Lee, D., Jin, X., Horvitz, H. R., & Nitabach, M. N. (2021). C. elegans discriminates colors to guide foraging. *Science*, 371(6533), 1059–1063.

Gibson, J. J. (1979). *The ecological approach to visual perception.* Psychology Press.

Giudice, N. A. (2018). Navigating without vision: Principles of blind spatial cognition. In D. R. Montello (Ed.), *Handbook of behavioral and cognitive geography* (pp. 260–289). Edward Elgar Publishing.

Goldberg, M. E., & Wurtz, R. H. (1972). Activity of superior colliculus in behaving monkey. II. Effect of attention on neuronal responses. *Journal of Neurophysiology*, 35(4), 560–574.

Goldin-Meadow, S. (2005). *Hearing gesture.* Harvard University Press.

Goodale, M. A. (2011). Transforming vision into action. *Vision Research*, 51(13), 1567–1587.

Goodale, M. A., & Humphrey, G. K. (1998). The objects of action and perception. *Cognition*, 67(1–2), 181–207.

Gopnik, A., O'Grady, S., Lucas, C. G. et al. (2017). Changes in cognitive flexibility and hypothesis search across human life history from childhood to adolescence to adulthood. *Proceedings of the National Academy of Sciences*, 114(30), 7892–7899.

Grossmann, T., Missana, M., & Krol, K. M. (2018). The neurodevelopmental precursors of altruistic behavior in infancy. *PLoS Biology*, 16(9), e2005281.

Guillery, R. W., & Sherman, S. M. (2002). Thalamic relay functions and their role in corticocortical communication: Generalizations from the visual system. *Neuron*, 33(2), 163–175.

Gunnar, M. R. (2017). Social buffering of stress in development: A career perspective. *Perspectives on Psychological Science*, 12(3), 355–373.

Gunnar, M. R., Fisher, P. A., & The Early Experience, Stress, and Prevention Network. (2006). Bringing basic research on early experience and stress neurobiology to bear on preventative interventions for neglected and mal-treated children. *Development and Psychopathology*, 18(3), 651–677.

Gunnar, M., & Quevedo, K. (2007). The neurobiology of stress and development. *Annual Review of Psychology*, 58, 145–173.

Gweon, H. (2021). Inferential social learning: Cognitive foundations of human social learning and teaching. *Trends in Cognitive Sciences*, 25(10), 896–910.

Hackel, L. M., Coppin, G., Wohl, M. J., & Van Bavel, J. J. (2018). From groups to grits. *Journal of Experimental Social Psychology*, 74, 270–280.

Hamlin, J. K. (2013). Moral judgment and action in preverbal infants and toddlers. *Current Directions in Psychological Science*, 22(3), 186–193.

Hare, B. (2017). Survival of the friendliest. *Annual Review of Psychology*, 68, 155–186.

Hare, B., & Tomasello, M. (2005). Human-like social skills in dogs? *Trends in Cognitive Science*, 9(9), 439–444.

Hare, B., Wobber, V., & Wrangham, R. (2012). The self-domestication hypothesis: Evolution of bonobo psychology is due to selection against aggression. *Animal Behaviour*, 83(3), 573–585.

Hayden, B. Y., & Niv, Y. (2021). The case against economic values in the orbitofrontal cortex (or anywhere else in the brain). *Behavioral Neuroscience*, 135(2), 192–201.

Heinrichs, M., Baumgartner, T., Kirschbaum, C., & Ehlert, U. (2003). Social support and oxytocin interact to suppress cortisol and subjective responses to psychosocial stress. *Biological Psychiatry*, 54(12), 1389–1398.

Herbert, J., & Schulkin, J. (2002). Neurochemical coding of adaptive responses in the limbic system. In D. Pfaff, A. Arnold, A. Etgen, S. Fahrbach, & R. Rubin (Eds.), *Hormones, Brain and Behavior* (pp. 659–689). Academic Press.

Heyes, C. (2019). What is cognition? *Current Biology*, 29(13), R611.

Heyes, C., Chater, N., & Dwyer, D. M. (2020). Sinking in: The peripheral Baldwinisation of human cognition. *Trends in Cognitive Sciences*, 24(11), 884–899.

House, E. L., & Pansky, B. (1960). *A functional approach to neuroanatomy.* McGraw-Hill.

Howell, W. H. (1916). *A textbook of physiology for medical students and physicians.* W.B. Saunders Co.

Hrdy, S. B. (2011). Mothers and others. *Natural History*, 110(4), 50–62.

Hubel, D. H., & Wiesel, T. N. (1959). Receptive fields of single neurones in the cat's striate cortex. *The Journal of Physiology*, 148(3), 574–591.

Hubel, D. H., & Wiesel, T. N. (1962). Receptive fields, binocular interaction and functional architecture in the cat's visual cortex. *The Journal of Physiology*, 160(1), 106–154.

Huebner, B. (2016) Implicit bias, reinforcement learning, and scaffolded moral cognition. In M. Brownstein & J. Saul (Eds.), *Implicit bias and philosophy: Vol. 1* (pp. 47–79). Oxford University Press.

Huebner, B. (2019). Picturing, signifying, and attending. *Belgrade Philosophical Annual*, (31), 7–40.

Hyde, P. S., & Knudsen, E. I. (2002). The optic tectum controls visually guided adaptive plasticity in the owl's auditory space map. *Nature*, 415(6867), 73–76.

Insel, T. R. (1992). Oxytocin—A neuropeptide for affiliation: Evidence from behavioral, receptor autoradiographic, and comparative studies. *Psychoneuroendocrinology*, 17(1), 3–35.

Itti, L., & Koch, C. (2000). A saliency-based search mechanism for overt and covert shifts of visual attention. *Vision Research*, 40(10–12), 1489–1506.

James, W. (1890). *The principles of psychology* (2 Vols.). Macmillan.

Kanwisher, N., & Yovel, G. (2006). The fusiform face area: A cortical region specialized for the perception of faces. *Philosophical Transactions of the Royal Society B: Biological Sciences*, 361(1476), 2109–2128.

Keijzer, F. (2013). The Sphex story: How the cognitive sciences kept repeating an old and questionable anecdote. *Philosophical Psychology*, 26(4), 502–519.

Kishida, K. T., Saez, I., Lohrenz, T. et al. (2016). Subsecond dopamine fluctuations in human striatum encode superposed error signals about actual and counterfactual reward. *Proceedings of the National Academy of Sciences*, 113(1), 200–205.

Koch, S. B., van Zuiden, M., Nawijn, L. et al. (2016). Intranasal oxytocin administration dampens amygdala reactivity towards emotional faces in male and female PTSD patients. *Neuropsychopharmacology*, 41(6), 1495–1504.

Krauzlis, R. J., Bollimunta, A., Arcizet, F., & Wang, L. (2014). Attention as an effect not a cause. *Trends in Cognitive Sciences*, 18(9), 457–464.

Krauzlis, R. J., Lovejoy, L. P., & Zénon, A. (2013). Superior colliculus and visual spatial attention. *Annual Review of Neuroscience*, 36, 165–182.

Kravitz, D. J., Saleem, K. S., Baker, C. I., & Mishkin, M. (2011). A new neural framework for visuospatial processing. *Nature Reviews Neuroscience*, 12(4), 217–230.

Krol, K. M., Moulder, R. G., Lillard, T. S., Grossmann, T., & Connelly, J. J. (2019a). Epigenetic dynamics in infancy and the impact of maternal engagement. *Science Advances*, 5(10), eaay0680.

Krol, K. M., Puglia, M. H., Morris, J. P., Connelly, J. J., & Grossmann, T. (2019b). Epigenetic modification of the oxytocin receptor gene is associated with emotion processing in the infant brain. *Developmental Cognitive Neuroscience*, 37, 100648.

Krosch, A. R., & Amodio, D. M. (2014) Economic scarcity alters the perception of race. *Proceedings of the National Academy of Sciences of the United States of America*, 111(25), 9079–9084.

Krubitzer, L. (2007). The magnificent compromise. *Neuron*, 56(2), 201–208.

Kryklywy, J. H., Ehlers, M. R., Anderson, A. K., & Todd, R. M. (2020). From architecture to evolution: Multisensory evidence of decentralized emotion. *Trends in Cognitive Sciences*, 24(11), 916–929.

Laland, K. N. (1993). Animal social learning. *Perspectives in Ethology*, 10, 249–277.

LeDoux, J. E., & Brown, R. (2017). A higher-order theory of emotional consciousness. *Proceedings of the National Academy of Sciences*, 114(10), E2016–E2025.

Lettvin, J. Y., Maturana, H. R., McCulloch, W. S., & Pitts, W. H. (1959). What the frog's eye tells the frog's brain. *Proceedings of the IRE*, 47(11), 1940–1951.

Levins, R. (1966). The strategy of model building in population biology. *American Scientist*, 54(4), 421–431.

Liljeholm, M., & O'Doherty, J. P. (2012). Contributions of the striatum to learning, motivation, and performance: An associative account. *Trends in Cognitive Sciences*, 16(9), 467–475.

Maley, C. J. (2021). The physicality of representation. *Synthese*, 199(5–6), 14725–14750.

Mandelbaum, E. (2019). Troubles with Bayesianism. *Mind & Language*, 34(2), 141–157.

Marder, E. (2012). Neuromodulation of neuronal circuits. *Neuron*, 76(1), 1–11.

Marler, P. (2000). Origins of music and speech: Insights from animals. In Wallin, N. L., Merker, B., & Brown, S. (Eds.), *The origins of music* (pp. 31–48). MIT Press.

Marr, D. (1982). *Vision: A computational investigation into the human representation and processing of visual information*. Henry Holt.

Marsh, A. A. (2016). Neural, cognitive, and evolutionary foundations of human altruism. *Wiley Interdisciplinary Reviews: Cognitive Science*, 7(1), 59–71.

Marsh, A. A., Henry, H. Y., Pine, D. S. et al. (2012). The influence of oxytocin administration on responses to infant faces and potential moderation by OXTR genotype. *Psychopharmacology*, 224(4), 469–476.

Marsh, N., Marsh, A. A., Lee, M. R., & Hurlemann, R. (2021). Oxytocin and the neurobiology of prosocial behavior. *The Neuroscientist*, 27(6), 604–619.

Martin, A. E. (2020). A compositional neural architecture for language. *Journal of Cognitive Neuroscience*, 32(8), 1407–1427.

Mauss, A. S., Vlasits, A., Borst, A., & Feller, M. (2017). Visual circuits for direction selectivity. *Annual Review of Neuroscience*, 40, 211–230.

Mayberry, R. I., & Kluender, R. (2018). Rethinking the critical period for language: New insights into an old question from American Sign Language. *Bilingualism: Language and Cognition*, 21(5), 886–905.

McComb, K., Shannon, G., Sayialel, K. N., & Moss, C. (2014). Elephants can determine ethnicity, gender, and age from acoustic cues in human voices. *Proceedings of the National Academy of Sciences*, 111(14), 5433–5438.

McEwen, B. S. (1998). Stress, adaptation, and disease. *Annals of the New York Academy of Sciences*, 840(1), 33–44.

McEwen, B. S. (2004) Protective and damaging effects of the mediators of stress and adaptation. In J. Schulkin (ed.), *Allostasis, homeostasis, and the costs of physiological adaptation* (pp. 65–98). Cambridge University Press.

McEwen, B. S. (2007). Physiology and neurobiology of stress and adaptation. *Physiological Reviews*, 87(3), 873–901.

McEwen, B. S. (2017). Allostasis and the epigenetics of brain and body health over the life course. *JAMA Psychiatry*, 74(6), 551–552.

McEwen, B. S., & Seeman, T. (1999). Protective and damaging effects of mediators of stress. *Annals of the New York Academy of Sciences*, 896(1), 30–47.

Merabet, L. B., Hamilton, R., Schlaug, G. et al. (2008). Rapid and reversible recruitment of early visual cortex for touch. *PLoS One*, 3(8), e3046.

Milner, A. D. (2017). How do the two visual streams interact with each other? *Experimental Brain Research*, 235(5), 1297–1308.

Milner, A. D., & Goodale, M. A. (2008). Two visual systems re-viewed. *Neuropsychologia*, 46(3), 774–785.

Montague, P. R. (2007). *Your brain is (almost) perfect: How we make decisions.* Penguin.

Montague, P. R., Dayan, P., & Sejnowski, T. J. (1996). A framework for mesencephalic dopamine systems based on predictive Hebbian learning. *Journal of Neuroscience*, 16(5), 1936–1947.

Mulroney, S. E., Woda, C. B., Halaihel, N. et al. (2004). Central control of renal sodium-phosphate (NaPi-2) transporters. *American Journal of Physiology-Renal Physiology*, 286(4), F647–F652.

Nagasawa, M., Mitsui, S., En, S. et al. (2015). Social evolution. Oxytocin-gaze positive loop and the coevolution of human-dog bonds. *Science*, 348(6232), 333–336.

Newport, E. L. (1988). Constraints on learning and their role in language acquisition. *Language Sciences*, 10(1), 147–172.

Newport, E. L. (2016). Statistical language learning: Computational, maturational, and linguistic constraints. *Language and Cognition*, 8(3), 447–461.

Newport, E. L. (2020). Children and adults as language learners: Rules, variation, and maturational change. *Topics in Cognitive Science*, 12(1), 153–169.

Norman, L J., & Thaler, L. (2019). Retinotopic-like maps of spatial sound in primary 'visual' cortex of blind human echolocators. *Proceedings of the Royal Society B*, 286(1912), 20191910.

Odenbaugh, J. (2003). Complex systems, trade-offs, and theoretical population biology: Richard Levin's "strategy of model building in population biology" revisited. *Philosophy of Science*, 70(5), 1496–1507.

O'Keeffe, J., & Nadel, L. (1978). *The hippocampus as a cognitive map.* Clarendon Press.

Op de Beeck, H. P., Pillet, I., & Ritchie, J. B. (2019). Factors determining where category-selective areas emerge in visual cortex. *Trends in Cognitive Sciences*, 23(9), 784–797.

O'Sullivan, S. (2017). *Is it all in your head? True stories of imaginary illness.* Other Press.

Pavlov, I. P. (1902). *The work of the digestive glands: Lectures by Professor JP Pavlow.* Tr. Into English by WH Thompson. C. Griffin.

Pavlov, I. (1927). *Conditioned reflexes: An investigation of the physiological activity of the cerebral cortex.* Oxford University Press

Pessoa, L. (2010). Emotion and cognition and the amygdala: From "what is it?" to "what's to be done?" *Neuropsychologia*, 48(12), 3416–3429.

Platt, M. L., & Pearson, J. M. (2016). Dopamine: Context and counterfactuals. *Proceedings of the National Academy of Sciences of the United States of America*, 113(1), 22–23.

Pollak, T. A., & Corlett, P. R. (2020). Blindness, psychosis, and the visual construction of the world. *Schizophrenia Bulletin*, 46(6), 1418–1425.

Power, M. L., & Schulkin, J. (2008). Anticipatory physiological regulation in feeding biology. *Appetite*, 50(2–3), 194–206.

Power, M. L., & Schulkin, J. (2017). *Milk: The biology of lactation.* JHU Press.

Powers, A. R. III, Kelley, M. S., & Corlett, P. R. (2017). Varieties of voice-hearing: Psychics and the psychosis continuum. *Schizophrenia Bulletin*, 43(1), 84–98.

Powers, S. I., Pietromonaco, P. R., Gunlicks, M., & Sayer, A. (2006). Dating couples' attachment styles and patterns of cortisol reactivity and recovery in response to a relationship conflict. *Journal of Personality and Social Psychology*, 90(4), 613–628.

Powley, T. L. (1977). The ventromedial hypothalamic syndrome, satiety, and a cephalic phase hypothesis. *Psychological Review*, 84(1), 89–126.

Purushothaman, G., Marion, R., Li, K., & Casagrande, V. A. (2012). Gating and control of primary visual cortex by pulvinar. *Nature Neuroscience*, 15(6), 905–912.

Prum, R. O. (2017). *The evolution of beauty*. Anchor.

Quintana, D. S., & Guastella, A. J. (2020). An allostatic theory of oxytocin. *Trends in Cognitive Sciences*, 24(7), 515–528.

Raglan, G. B., Schmidt, L. A., & Schulkin, J. (2017). The role of glucocorticoids and corticotropin-releasing hormone regulation on anxiety symptoms and response to treatment. *Endocrine Connections*, 6(2), R1–R7.

Railton, P. (2017). At the core of our capacity to act for a reason: The affective system and evaluative model-based learning and control. *Emotion Review*, 9(4), 335–342.

Rakoczy, H., & Schmidt, M. F. (2013). The early ontogeny of social norms. *Child Development Perspectives*, 7(1), 17–21.

Ramón y Cajal, S. (1899). *Comparative study of the sensory areas of the human cortex*. Clark University.

Reader, S. M., & Laland, K. N. (2002). Social intelligence, innovation, and enhanced brain size in primates. *Proceedings of the National Academy of Sciences of the United States of America*, 99(7), 4436–4441.

Reich, L., Szwed, M., Cohen, L., & Amedi, A. (2011). A ventral visual stream reading center independent of visual experience. *Current Biology*, 21(5), 363–368.

Rescorla, R. A. (1980). Simultaneous and successive associations in sensory preconditioning. *Journal of Experimental Psychology: Animal Behavior Processes*, 6(3), 207–216.

Rescorla, R. A. (1988). Pavlovian conditioning: It's not what you think it is. *American Psychologist*, 43(3), 151–160.

Rescorla, R. A., & Wagner, A. R. (1972). A theory of Pavlovian conditioning. In A. H. Black & W. F. Prokasy (Eds.), *Classical conditioning II: Current research and theory* (pp. 64–99). Appleton Century Crofts.

Richter, C. P. (1943). Total self-regulatory functions in animals and human beings. *Harvey Lecture Series*, 38, 63–103.

Richter, C. P. (1953). Behavior cycles in man and animals. *Science*, 117(3044), 470.

Richter, C. P. (1956). Salt appetite of mammals: Its dependence on instinct and metabolism. *L'instinct dans Ie comportement des animaux et de l'homme. Paris*, 577–629.

Ritzel, K., & Gallo, T. (2020). Behavior change in urban mammals. *Frontiers in Ecology and Evolution*, 8, 393.

Rosen, J. B., & Schulkin, J. (1998). From normal fear to pathological anxiety. *Psychological Review*, 105(2), 325–350.

Rosen, J. B., & Schulkin, J. (2004). Adaptive fear, allostasis, and the pathology of anxiety and depression. In J. Schulkin (Ed.), *Allostasis, homeostasis, and the costs of physiological adaptation* (pp. 164–227). Cambridge University Press.

Rozin, P. (1990). Acquisition of stable food preferences. *Nutrition Reviews*, 48(2), 106–113.

Rozin, P., & Kalat, J. W. (1971). Specific hungers and poison avoidance as adaptive specializations of learning. *Psychological Review*, 78(6), 459–486.

Rozin, P. N., & Schulkin, J. (1990). Food selection. In E. M. Stricker (Ed.), *Neurobiology of food and fluid intake* (pp. 297–328). Plenum Press.

Sapolsky, R. (1996). Why stress is bad for your brain. *Science*, 273(5276), 749–750.

Sapolsky, R. (2005). The influence of social hierarchy on primate health. *Science*, 308(5722), 648–652.

Sapolsky, R., Romero, L. M., & Munck, A. U. (2000). How do glucocorticosteroids influence stress responses? *Endocrinology Review*, 21(1), 55–89.

Schulkin, J. (1991). *Sodium hunger: The search for a salty taste*. Cambridge University Press.

Schulkin, J. (2004). *Allostasis, homeostasis, and the costs of physiological adaptation*. Cambridge University Press.

Schulkin, J. (2006). Angst and the amygdala. *Dialogues in Clinical Neuroscience*, 8(4), 407–416.

Schulkin, J. (2011). *Adaptation and well-being*. Cambridge University Press.

Schulkin, J. (2015). *Pragmatism and the search for coherence in neuroscience*. Springer.

Schulkin, J., McEwen, B. S., & Gold, P. W. (1994). Allostasis, amygdala, and anticipatory angst. *Neuroscience & Biobehavioral Reviews*, 18(3), 385–396.

Schulkin, J., & Sterling, P. (2019). Allostasis: A brain-centered, predictive mode of physiological regulation. *Trends in Neurosciences*, 42(10), 740–752.

Schulkin, J., Thompson, B. L., & Rosen, J. B. (2003). Demythologizing the emotions: Adaptation, cognition, and visceral representations of emotion in the nervous system. *Brain and Cognition*, 52(1), 15–23.

Schultz, W. (2010). Dopamine signals for reward value and risk: Basic and recent data. *Behavioral and Brain Functions* 6(24). https://bit.ly/3s9fKEy.

Selfridge, O. (1959). Pandemonium: A paradigm for learning. Paper presented at Proceedings of the Symposium on Mechanisation of Thought Processes, National Physical Laboratory, Teddington, November 1958 (Vol. 1, pp. 513–526). HMSO.

Seligman, M. E. (1971). Phobias and preparedness. *Behavior Therapy*, 2(3), 307–320.

Serre, T., Oliva, A., & Poggio, T. (2007). A feedforward architecture accounts for rapid categorization. *Proceedings of the National Academy of Sciences of the United States of America*, 104(15), 6424–6429.

Seth, A. (2021). *Being you: A new science of consciousness*. Penguin.

Seth, A. K., & Tsakiris, M. (2018). Being a beast machine: The somatic basis of selfhood. *Trends in Cognitive Sciences*, 22(11), 969–981.

Sharpe, M. J., Batchelor, H. M., Mueller, L. E. et al. (2020). Dopamine transients do not act as model-free prediction errors during associative learning. *Nature Communications*, 11(1), 1–10.

Shepard, R. N. (1984). Ecological constraints on internal representation. *Psychological Review*, 91(4), 414–447.

Shilton, D., Breski, M., Dor, D., & Jablonka, E. (2020). Human social evolution: Self-domestication or self-control? *Frontiers in Psychology*, 11, 134.

Shine, J. M, O'Callaghan, C., Wainstein, G. et al. (2022). Understanding the effects of serotonin in the brain through its role in the gastrointestinal tract. *Brain*, 145(9), 2967–2981.

Shutts, K., Kinzler, K. D., & DeJesus, J. M. (2013). Understanding infants' and children's social learning about foods: Previous research and new prospects. *Developmental Psychology*, 49(3), 419–425.

Silk, J. B. (2007). The adaptive value of sociality in mammalian groups. *Philosophical Transactions of the Royal Society B: Biological Sciences*, 362(1480), 539–559.

Silk, J., Cheney, D., & Seyfarth, R. (2013). A practical guide to the study of social relationships. *Evolutionary Anthropology: Issues, News, and Reviews*, 22(5), 213–225.

Silver, M., & Sabini, J. (2012). Sincerity: Feelings and constructions in making a self. In K. J. Gergen & K. E. Davis (Eds.), *The social construction of the person* (pp. 191–201). Springer.

Starling, E. H. (1905). The Croonian lectures. *Lancet*, 26, 339–341.

Sterelny, K. (2021). *The Pleistocene social contract: Culture and cooperation in human evolution*. Oxford University Press.

Sterling, P., & Eyer, J. (1988). Allostasis: A new paradigm to explain arousal pathology. In S. Fisher & J. Reason (Eds.), *Handbook of life stress, cognition and health* (pp. 629–649). John Wiley & Sons.

Sterling, P., & Laughlin, S. (2015). *Principles of neural design*. MIT Press.

Sterzer, P., Adams, R. A., Fletcher, P. et al. (2018). The predictive coding account of psychosis. *Biological Psychiatry*, 84(9), 634–643.

Stokes, D., Matthen, M., & Biggs, S. (Eds.) (2015). *Perception and its modalities*. Oxford University Press.

Striem-Amit, E., Ovadia-Caro, S., Caramazza, A. et al. (2015). Functional connectivity of visual cortex in the blind follows retinotopic organization principles. *Brain*, 138(6), 1679–1695.

Sykes, R. W. (2020). *Kindred: Neanderthal life, love, death and art*. Bloomsbury.

Swanson, L. W., & Petrovich, G. D. (1998). What is the amygdala? *Trends in Neurosciences*, 21(8), 323–331.

Takagi, S., Saito, A., Arahori, M. et al. (2022). Cats learn the names of their friend cats in their daily lives. *Scientific Reports*, 12(1), 6155.

Talmi, D., Ziegler, M., Hawksworth, J. et al. (2013) Emotional stimuli exert parallel effects on attention and memory. *Cognition & Emotion*, 27(3), 530–538.

Tamietto, M., Cauda, F., Corazzini, L. L. et al. (2010). Collicular vision guides nonconscious behavior. *Journal of Cognitive Neuroscience*, 22(5), 888–902.

Tenenbaum, J. B., Kemp, C., Griffiths, T. L., & Goodman, N. D. (2011). How to grow a mind: Statistics, structure, and abstraction. *Science*, 331(6022), 1279–1285.

Theriault, J., Young, L., & Barrett, L. F. (2021). The sense of should: A biologically-based model of social pressure. *Physics of Life Reviews*, 36, 100–136.

Thompson, E. (1995). Colour vision, evolution, and perceptual content. *Synthese*, 104(1), 1–32.

Tinbergen, N. (1951). *The study of instinct*. Oxford University Press.

Tinbergen, N. (1953). *Social behaviour in animals*. Psychology Press.

Todd, R. M., & Manaligod, M. G. (2018). Implicit guidance of attention: The priority state space framework. *Cortex*, 102, 121–138.

Tomasello, M. (2009). *The cultural origins of human cognition*. Harvard University Press.

Tomasello, M, Melis, A. P., Tennie, C., Wyman, E., & Herrmann, E. (2012). Two key steps in the evolution of cooperation. *Current Anthropology*, 53(6), 673–692.

Tschantz, A., Barca, L., Maisto, D. et al. (2021). Simulating homeostatic, allostatic and goal-directed forms of interoceptive control using Active Inference. *Biological Psychology*, 169, 108266.

Ungerleider, L. G., & Pessoa, L. (2018). What and where pathways. *Scholarpedia*, 3(11), 5342.

Vallorani, A., Fu, X., Morales, S. et al. (2021). Variable- and person-centered approaches to affect-biased attention in infancy reveal unique relations with infant negative affect and maternal anxiety. *Scientific Reports*, 11(1), 1–14.

Vyas, A., Mitra, R., Rao, B. S., & Chattarji, S. (2002). Chronic stress induces contrasting patterns of dendritic remodeling in hippocampal and amygdaloid neurons. *Journal of Neuroscience*, 22(15), 6810–6818.

Wang, Y. C., Bianciardi, M., Chanes, L., & Satpute, A. B. (2020). Ultra-high field fMRI of human superior colliculi activity during affective visual processing. *Scientific Reports*, 10(1), 1–7.

Warneken, F., & Tomasello, M. (2006). Altruistic helping in human infants and young chimpanzees. *Science*, 311(5765), 1301–1303.

Warneken, F., Hare, B., Melis, A. P., Hanus, D., & Tomasello, M. (2007). Spontaneous altruism by chimpanzees and young children. *PLoS Biology*, 5(7), e184.

Waterhouse, B. D., & Navarra, R. L. (2019). The locus coeruleus-norepinephrine system and sensory signal processing: A historical review and current perspectives. *Brain Research*, 1709, 1–15.

Wilcoxon, H. C., Dragoin, W. B., & Kral, P. A. (1971). Illness-induced aversions in rat and quail. *Science*, 171(3973), 826–828.

Wilkins, A. S., Wrangham, R. W., & Fitch, W. T. (2014). The "domestication syndrome" in mammals. *Genetics*, 197(3), 795–808.

Wittig, R. M., Crockford, C., Lehman, J. et al. (2008). Focused grooming networks and stress alleviation in wild female baboons. *Hormones & Behavior*, 54(1), 170–177.

Wolf, G. (1969). Innate mechanisms for regulation of sodium intake. *Olfaction and Taste*, 3, 548–553.

Woods, S. C., Vasselli, J. R., Kaestner, E. et al. (1977). Conditioned insulin secretion and meal feeding in rats. *Journal of Comparative and Physiological Psychology*, 91(1), 128–133.

Wrangham, R. (2019). *The goodness paradox*. Pantheon.

Wurtz, R. H. (2009). Recounting the impact of Hubel and Wiesel. *The Journal of Physiology*, 587(12), 2817–2823.

Yang, C. (2016). *The price of linguistic productivity: How children learn to break the rules of language*. MIT Press.

Yehuda, R. (2002). Post-traumatic stress disorder. *New England Journal of Medicine*, 346(2), 108–114.

Yehuda, R., & LeDoux, J. (2007). Response variation following trauma: A translational neuroscience approach to understanding PTSD. *Neuron*, 56(1), 19–32.

Zhaoping, L. (2016). From the optic tectum to the primary visual cortex: Migration through evolution of the saliency map for exogenous attentional guidance. *Current Opinion in Neurobiology*, 40, 94–102.

Zhuang, C., Yan, S., Nayebi, A. et al. (2021). Unsupervised neural network models of the ventral visual stream. *Proceedings of the National Academy of Sciences*, 118(3), e2014196118.

Cambridge Elements ☰

Philosophy of Mind

Keith Frankish

The University of Sheffield

Keith Frankish is a philosopher specializing in philosophy of mind, philosophy of psychology, and philosophy of cognitive science. He is the author of *Mind and Supermind* (Cambridge University Press, 2004) and *Consciousness* (2005), and has also edited or coedited several collections of essays, including *The Cambridge Handbook of Cognitive Science* (Cambridge University Press, 2012), *The Cambridge Handbook of Artificial Intelligence* (Cambridge University Press, 2014) (both with William Ramsey), and *Illusionism as a Theory of Consciousness* (2017).

About the Series

This series provides concise, authoritative introductions to contemporary work in philosophy of mind, written by leading researchers and including both established and emerging topics. It provides an entry point to the primary literature and will be the standard resource for researchers, students, and anyone wanting a firm grounding in this fascinating field.

Cambridge Elements ≡

Philosophy of Mind

Elements in the Series

A full series listing is available at: www.cambridge.org/EPMI

Printed in the United States
by Baker & Taylor Publisher Services